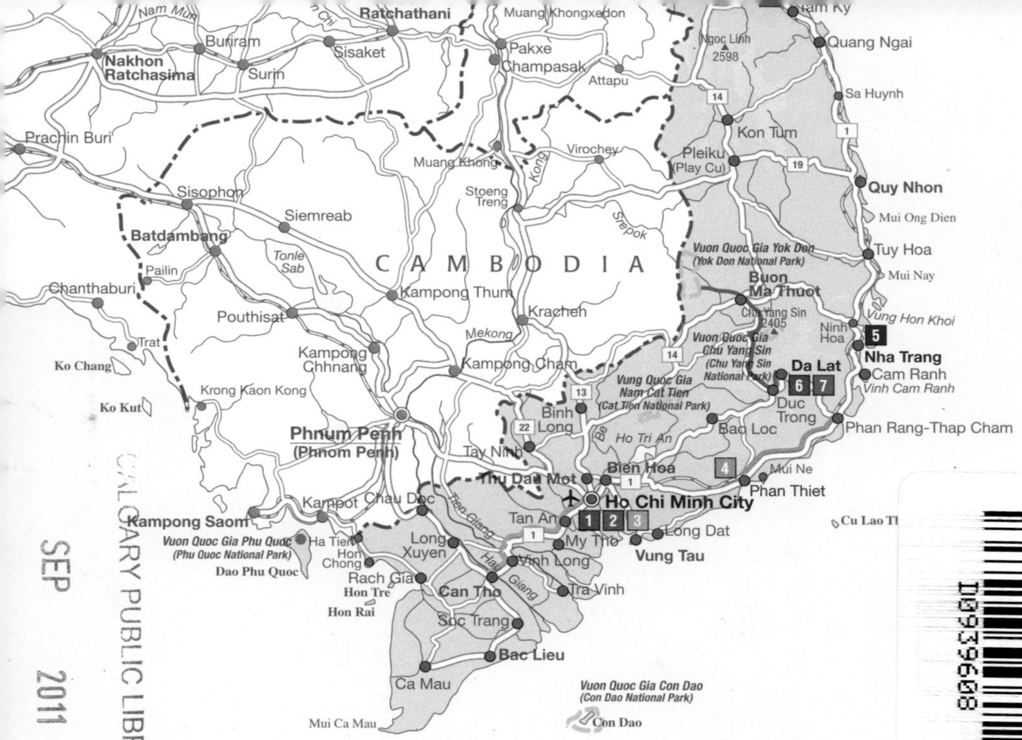

Vietnam

Tours

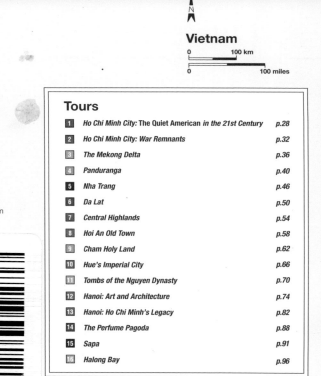

INSIGHT GUIDES

VIETNAM

StepbyStep

APA PUBLICATIONS
Part of the Langenscheidt Publishing Group

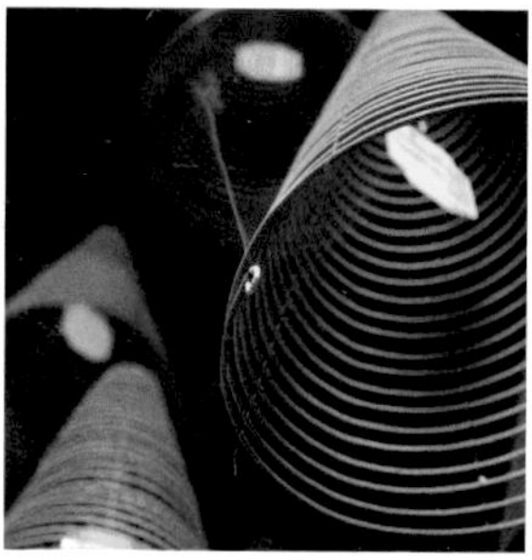

CONTENTS

ABOUT THIS BOOK

Above: Do Lat Palace; Trang Tien Bridge in Hue; Hang Cot Street in Hanoi; the highest peak in Vietnam, Mount Fansipan; the limestone karsts and islands of Halong Bay.

This *Step by Step Guide* has been produced by the editors of Insight Guides, whose books have set the standard for visual travel guides since 1970. With top-quality photography and authoritative recommendations, this guidebook brings you the very best of Vietnam in a series of 16 tailor-made tours.

WALKS AND TOURS

The tours in the book provide something to suit all budgets, tastes and trip lengths. As well as covering Vietnam's two major cities, Hanoi and Ho Chi Minh City, the routes track the interior of the country, from the Mekong Delta through the Central Highlands and on to Halong Bay. There are walking tours of the main cities and ancient sights as well as regional multi-day tours. The tours embrace a range of interests, so whether you are a beachcomer, historian or gourmet, you will find an option to suit.

We recommend that you read the whole of a tour before setting out. This should help you to familiarise yourself with the route and enable you to plan where to stop for refreshments – options for this are shown in the 'Food and Drink' boxes, recognisable by the knife-and-fork sign, on most pages.

For our pick of the walks by theme, consult Recommended Tours For... *(see pp.6–7)*.

OVERVIEW

The tours are set in context by this introductory section, giving an overview of the country to set the scene, plus background information on food, shopping, entertainment and festivals. A history timeline highlights the key events that have shaped Vietnam over the centuries.

DIRECTORY

Also supporting the tours is a Directory chapter, comprising a user-friendly, clearly organised A–Z of practical information, our pick of where to stay while you are in the area and select restaurant listings; these eateries complement the more low-key options that feature within the tours and are intended to offer a wider choice for evening dining. Also included here are some nightlife listings.

The Author

Adam Bray has contributed to nearly 20 guidebooks on Vietnam and neighbouring countries in Southeast Asia. These include Insight Guide Vietnam, Berlitz Pocket Guide Vietnam, Insight Pocket Guide Vietnam and Insight Guide Southeast Asia. Adam has been based in Phan Thiet, Vietnam, since 2003 and speaks Vietnamese and a bit of Cambodian and Cham. He is a specialist in minority cultures, present and past, and has uncovered a number of ancient Cham temple ruins in his home province. Visit his websites at www.muinebeach.net and www.fisheggtree.com for regular updates on his adventures.

Some of the tours in this book were originally conceived by Samantha Coomber and Lucy Forwood.

Margin Tips

Shopping tips, historical facts, handy hints and information on activities help visitors to make the most of their time in Vietnam.

Feature Boxes

Notable topics are highlighted in these special boxes.

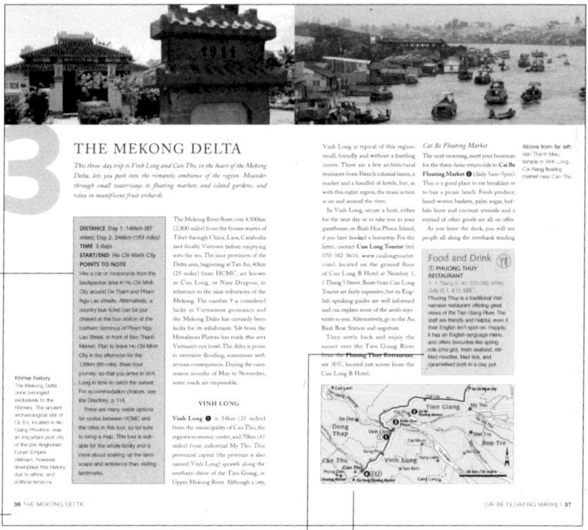

Key Facts Box

This box gives details of the distance covered on the tour, plus an estimate of how long it should take. It also states where the route starts and finishes, and gives key travel information such as which days are best to do the route or handy transport tips.

Footers

Look here for the tour name, a map reference and the main attraction on the double-page.

Food and Drink

Recommendations of where to stop for refreshment are given in these boxes. The numbers prior to each restaurant/café name link to references in the main text. Restaurants in the Food and Drink boxes are plotted on the maps.

The $ signs at the end of each entry reflect the approximate cost of a meal for one including up to three dishes and a drink.

$$$$	Over US$10
$$$	US$6–$10
$$	US$2.50–5
$	Under US$2.50

Route Map

Detailed cartography shows the tour clearly plotted with numbered dots. For more detailed mapping, see the pull-out map slotted inside the back cover.

ART & ARCHITECTURE

Whether it's ancient Vietnamese temples, Chinese shop houses or French colonial villas, great architecture is everywhere in Vietnam. Explore much of it in HCMC (tour 1), Hoi An Old Town (tour 8), Hue's Imperial City (tour 10) and Hanoi (tour 12).

RECOMMENDED TOURS FOR...

BEACHCOMBING

Vietnam's coastline is extensive, and while most cities on travellers' itineraries have a beachfront, tours 4 and 5 through Panduranga and Nha Trang offer visitors the best of Vietnam's sunbathing and water sports.

CHAMPA KINGDOM

The Champa Kingdom controlled all of central Vietnam for over a century. Explore their temple ruins, ancient citadels, refined sculptures and thriving modern culture in tours 4 and 9.

CUISINE

Vietnamese cuisine is deservedly the subject of much international attention. Be sure to visit Hanoi (tours 12 and 13), Hue (tour 10) and HCMC (tours 1 and 2) for the best selection of cuisine.

HILL TRIBES

Vietnam has a vast, mountainous interior inhabited by most of its 54 recognised ethnic minorities. Meet some of them and learn about their traditional lifestyles in tours 6, 7 and 15.

MODERN VIETNAM

Vietnam has undergone a tremendous growth spurt over the last decade, and HCMC seems to get a makeover every other year. Partake in urban Vietnam's grand nightlife, shopping and entertainment with walks and tours in HCMC (tours 1 and 2), Hanoi (tours 12 and 13) and Nha Trang (tour 5).

OFF THE BEATEN PATH

If you are keen to get off the tourist trail and experience something especially unique and memorable, Vietnam still offers lots of regions less overrun by the tourist crowds. Get off the beaten path and see the 'real Vietnam' in the Mekong Delta (tour 3), the Central Highlands (tour 7) and Panduranga (tour 4).

OUTDOORS

Ecotourism is the least developed aspect of Vietnam's tourism industry, which is a surprise given its beautiful landscapes. Get a fill of the country's natural splendours in tours 7, 14, 15 and 16.

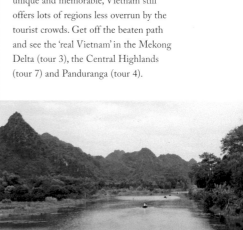

TRANQUILLITY

Vietnam is a noisy country with crowded cities, yet a few spots, especially temples, offer a meditative ambience in beautiful surroundings. Those seeking some peace and quiet away from the buzz of the hustle and bustle should try tours 7, 10, 11 and 14.

WAR HISTORY

Vietnam has been caught up in war and conflict during most of the nation's history. The last war with America is still the one on most people's minds. Get a glimpse into Vietnam's troubled past with tours 1, 2 and 13.

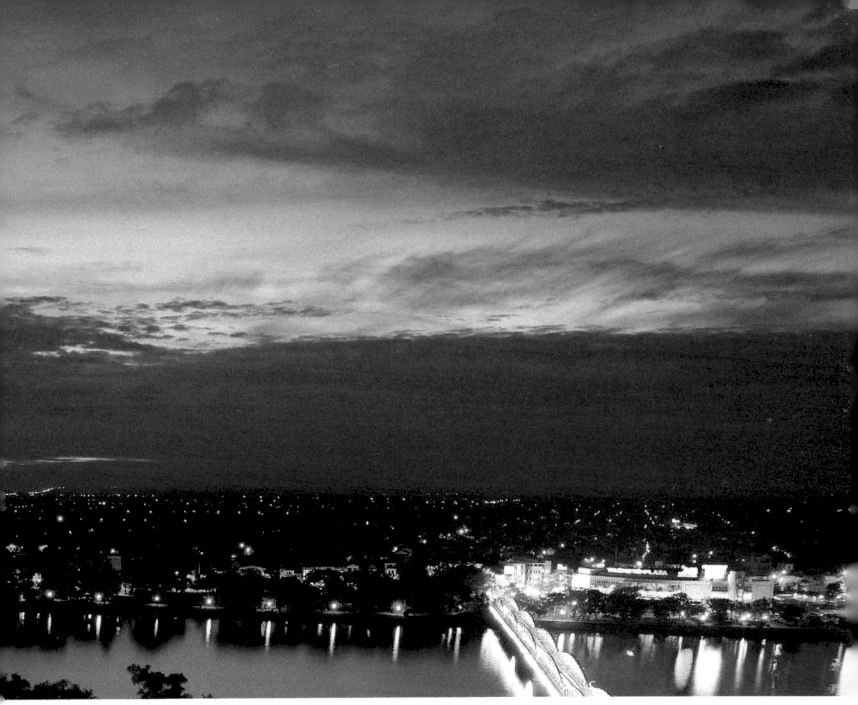

OVERVIEW

An overview of Vietnamese geography, customs and culture, plus illuminating background information on food and drink, shopping, festivals, entertainment and history.

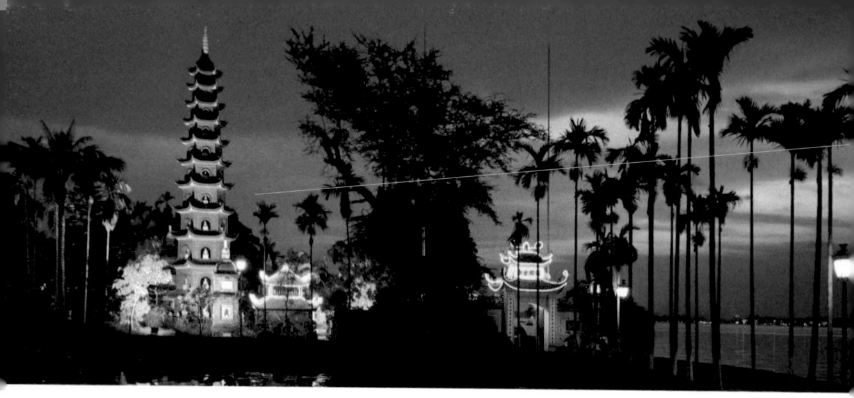

INTRODUCTION

21st-century Vietnam is thriving economically and as a tourist destination thanks to freedoms introduced over the past two decades. Visitors are flocking to Ho Chi Minh City, Hanoi and other vibrant coastal cities to explore this country with its infamous history, diverse culture and modern dynamism.

Above: Dong Xuan Market is the oldest in Hanoi.

For more than 2,000 years Vietnam's development as a nation has been marked by its proximity to China. No country in Southeast Asia is culturally closer to China than Vietnam, and no other country in the region has spent so long fighting off Chinese domination. Likewise, the Vietnamese spent more than a millennium pushing against the Champa Kingdom to the south, until it was finally dissolved and its territory taken over by Emperor Minh Mang in the early 1800s.

There is a modern slogan: *Vietnam is a country, not a war*. However, for 35 years after World War II, Vietnam was almost synonymous with war, first with the French, then the Americans, and finally the Khmer Rouge, with Chinese reprisals.

Perhaps because of the long years of rivalries, Vietnam has developed a powerful sense of national identity, possessing a unique cultural heritage that is both strongly Sinicised and also distinctively Southeast Asian.

In the roughly 20 years since Vietnam first began to open up to the outside world, great changes have been made. Standards of living have risen dramatically, communications have improved and most of the country is now accessible. Still more importantly, as the government has relaxed, so have the Vietnamese people. Once characterised by shyness or insecurity, which sometimes manifested itself in a cool or reserved manner, the Vietnamese are now amazingly open, friendly and often eager to meet foreign travellers.

GEOGRAPHY AND LAYOUT

Northern Vietnam is anchored by Hanoi, an ancient city established 1,000 years ago. Beyond Hanoi, the provinces of the vast Red River Delta reflect the traditional agricultural culture on which the economy is based. The surrounding mountain regions, populated by hill tribes, ascend towards Laos in the west and north towards China.

Southwards, following the historical movement of the Viet people, is a chain of coastal provinces washed by the South China Sea. In the centre is Hue, the old imperial city of the Nguyen Dynasty, and vestiges of the Cham holy land at My Son.

In the south, the former capital of Saigon, now known as Ho Chi Minh City (HCMC), remains the country's economic and pop culture capital, and gateway to the Mekong. Where Hanoi is quiet, Ho Chi Minh is frenetic. If Hanoi is a city of earth tones, Ho Chi Minh is neon, all lit up in gaudy lights.

Getting around Vietnam is becoming much easier with improved roads, airports and a reliable rail system. Still, neither Hanoi nor Ho Chi Minh City offers a viable mass urban transport system for visitors, and in both cities the best bet is to taxi from place to place.

HISTORICAL ARCHITECTURE

A curious blend of Chinese and French styles has influenced architecture in Hanoi, most of which dates from the last two centuries; there are some particularly great examples of colonial style in the French Quarter, while the city's temples and pagodas display the melding of Sino-Vietnamese design elements.

In the ancient port town of Hoi An is a blend of Chinese, Japanese and French influences, creating a unique and cohesive architectural style. Further southwest in the mountain resort of Da Lat an abundance of French colonial architecture has been preserved due to the absence of military action there during the Indochina wars.

The assimilation of external historical elements in Ho Chi Minh City has resulted in Vietnamese, Soviet, French, Western and Chinese architectural influences and a contrasting mishmash of edifices. Similarly to Hanoi, French colonial is still the city's loveliest architectural legacy, remaining highly visible today.

POPULATION

About 86 percent of Vietnam's population are ethnic Viets, also known as Kinh. They originated in southern China, where communities persist in an ancient culture and lifestyle. The

Above from far left: Tran Quoc Pagoda in Hanoi; countryside around the village of Kenh Ga.

Below: Hanoi's Old East Gate.

When to visit
Determining the 'best time to visit Vietnam' is entirely subjective, since each region has its own weather patterns. Furthermore, the rainy season is not necessarily a bad time to visit, as showers are usually a brief afternoon interlude, and can be planned around. The rains have the added benefit of cooling the temperatures and initiating the growth of foliage and flora.

remaining 14 percent of the population are officially divided among 54 ethnic groups, although in reality there are probably hundreds of different tribes.

Vietnam's 1 million ethnic Chinese (Hoa) constitute the most important ethnic minority. The ancestors of the Hoa came principally from the southern Chinese provinces of Guangxi, Guangdong, Fujian, Zhejiang and Taiwan.

The Cham inhabit Ninh Thuan and Binh Thuan Province (the former Cham province of Panduranga), as well as parts of the Mekong Delta (and eastern Cambodia). Once masters of much of central Vietnam and portions of Cambodia and Laos, they now number around 150,000 within Vietnam. The coastal Cham are predominantly Hindu (Balamon), while those of the Mekong Delta are Muslim (Bani).

Ethnic minorities in the mountains of central Vietnam form another significant group. Called *montagnards* by the French, they include Muong, Ma, K'ho, Ede, Jarai, Bahnar and Sedang. The highlands of the north are home to numerous minorities as well, including the Tay, Tai, Hmong, Dao and Nung.

Below: Diamond Plaza shopping centre, HCMC.

CLIMATE

The south has two seasons; wet and dry. The rains arrive in mid-May and leave in mid-December. Between these months it may rain fiercely for about one hour a day, normally in the afternoon or early evening. Late February to late April are the hottest months, with temperatures well into the mid-30s°C (86°F).

Central Vietnam from Da Nang to Nha Trang has its own weather patterns due to the monsoons: the dry season is from January to September, with the rainfall from October to mid-January. The seasons are not as pronounced here, however, and it can rain at any time of the year. Hue, the wettest city in Vietnam, as well as the Western Highlands, tends to get a lot of rain throughout the year.

The north experiences four seasons. The summer months from May to September are almost always hot and humid, with the most rainfall

during this period. Winter, from late December to early March, is grey, drizzly and cool.

LOCAL CUSTOMS

Most banks, public services and state-run offices work Monday to Friday, opening between 7.30 and 8.30am, and closing between 4 and 5pm, with a lunch break between 11.30 and 1.30. Museums roughly follow the same hours, but generally close on Monday. Tourist-orientated shops work a seven-day week from 8am to 9pm. Markets open as early as 5.30am, winding down by lunchtime. Only very large markets in city centres stay active all day.

Tourists staying in hotels and guesthouses do not need to register with the police directly. When you check in at reception the staff will take your passport to the police for registration. They will return it to you the next morning.

POLITICS AND LOCAL ECONOMY

The Socialist Republic of Vietnam (the country's full title) is a one-party communist state. The 1986 Doi Moi (Renovation) policies initiated a move toward a 'socialist-oriented market economy' but did little to shake up the monopoly on ideology and power of the leadership in charge. However, there has been a vast economic revolution and speedy national development with the advent (though incomplete) of privatisation. Foreign investment is key to Vietnam's growing economy with, ironically, the United States now taking the lead as Vietnam's largest business and trade partner.

The economic impact of Viet Kieu (overseas Vietnamese) cannot be understated. Originally fleeing the country as refugees after the fall of Saigon, they resettled in Western countries (particularly the United States and Australia) and began sending money to their relatives left behind in Vietnam. These remittances are now estimated to average an astounding US$7 billion per year. Realising the danger of losing this revenue as the Viet Kieu age, the government has recently begun relaxing punitive regulations and encouraging Viet Kieu to return, invest and retire here.

Above from far left: beautiful Bai Sao Beach on Phu Quoc island; Lang Son in the northeast; evidence of higher disposable incomes.

Thorny Issues

Vietnam currently struggles with a number of taboo political issues, including bauxite mining by Chinese migrant workers in the Central Highlands, political unrest among Central Highlands minority groups, land rights of Catholic churches and persecution of Protestant groups. The advent of internet social media created a new vehicle for disseminating information and protesting about these issues, which led to stern reaction from the government. A crackdown on internet 'abuses of freedom' was initiated in 2008, leading to the arrest of bloggers and blocking of websites, including Facebook in 2009.

FOOD AND DRINK

The essence of Vietnamese cuisine is the pursuit of perfect harmony and balance among the five essential flavours: sweet, sour, savoury, spicy and bitter. This balance may be achieved within a single dish or through an entire banquet, but the experience is always memorable.

Vietnamese cuisine is light, delicious, generally very healthy, and comes in endless variety. Rice *(com)* is the staple, topped with meat, fish and vegetables. Many Vietnamese believe that a proper meal must always include rice. Thus, one of the most common questions in Vietnamese following a greeting is, '*Ban an com chua?*' (Have you eaten rice yet?). Fresh, raw herbs, subtly spicy broths, separate dipping sauces, and condiments are prevalent in Vietnamese cuisine. Most sauces are made with a base of *nuoc mam* (a pungent fish sauce).

Modern Vietnamese cuisine borrows heavily from Chinese, but also has significant influence from French, and some elements introduced by Portuguese, Khmer and indigenous Cham. The Chinese contributed stir-fries, spring rolls, noodles and soy sauce; the French brought baguettes, pastries, pâté and dairy products. Together with the Portuguese, the French also introduced many of Vietnam's staples, including coffee, black pepper, potatoes and tapioca. Curries and many other spices probably came to Vietnam through the Cham and Khmer (both heavily influenced by Indian culture themselves).

Below: international dishes, such as these tacos, are increasingly found in Ho Chi Minh City.

LOCAL CUISINES

Vietnam has three main culinary regions: the north (Hanoi), the south (HCMC) and the centre (Hue and Hoi An), each with differences in both their main dishes and snacks, as well as their use of ingredients and methods of cooking.

The unofficial national dish, *pho* (rice noodle soup) is the most common street food, especially in Hanoi. Usually eaten for breakfast, it makes a tasty meal at any time of the day. A hot, aromatic broth is poured over noodles topped with either slivers of rare beef *(bo)* or chicken *(ga)*. In the south chillies, lemon, sauces and herbs are added. *Chao tom* is another northern delicacy: finely minced shrimp baked on a stick of sugar cane, eaten with lettuce, cucumber, coriander *(cilantro)* and mint, and dipped in fish sauce. A Hanoi favourite is *bun cha*, charcoal-grilled pork meatballs served in a light broth, accompanied by cold vermicelli noodles, lettuce and herbs.

Hue, a city associated with Buddhism, is famous for its vegetarian cuisine as well as the food of the royal court. As the seat of Vietnam's last royal dynasty, many of the local dishes were once reserved only for the king. Typical Hue specialities include *bun bo* – fried beef and noodles served with coriander, onion, garlic, cucumber, chilli peppers and tomato paste – as well as *banh khoai*, a potato pancake.

As the country's modern commercial capital, Ho Chi Minh City is a place where food from every region can be found in bountiful supply. The city's most celebrated local dish is *banh xeo*, a sizzling crêpe pan-fried with pork, shrimps and bean sprouts, which is folded over and cooked to a crispy golden brown. Other popular Vietnamese dishes include *cha gio* (known as *nem Saigon* in the north): 'spring rolls' of minced pork, prawn, crabmeat, mushrooms and vegetables wrapped in thin rice paper and then deep-fried. These are then rolled in a lettuce leaf with fresh mint and other herbs, and dipped in a sweet fish sauce known as *nuoc cham*.

Above from far left: *rau thom*, a platter of raw herbs served as an accompaniment to the meal; Hoi An cuisine.

WHERE TO EAT

Street Food

The most authentic (and best) Vietnamese food is found along street sides, down alleys and inside local markets, where stall keepers specialise in just one dish and serve the freshest food. Look out for signs over stalls with steaming cauldrons surrounded by toy-sized plastic chairs. Try to arrive in local street-food eateries before 9am for breakfast, by noon for lunch and 6–7pm for dinner, as food can run out early. Compared to other countries, it's still relatively inexpensive in Vietnam to dine out, and street food is astoundingly good value. Expect to pay no more than $1–2 per person on the street.

Diners and Canteens

Basic indoor eateries, sometimes served out of homes or shops, normally offer only one or two house specialities – noodle soups or rice meals with a selection of meat and vegetables. The differences from street food are found

Safe street food
When eating street food and at small canteens and diners, try to select a venue that is crowded. This not only suggests that the food tastes good, but is also fresh. Empty restaurants are more likely to serve unrefrigerated leftovers.

in the slightly higher prices, better seating arrangements, more reliable opening hours and better food hygiene. Usually diners and canteens are open for breakfast and dinner, but most are closed for lunch, as Vietnamese tend to go home during their lunch hour. The exceptions are takeaways serving *com binh danh* (popular rice). Sometimes the selection in the morning is different from the evening offering at any given venue. Canteens usually have no menus, and often no beverages other than free iced tea.

Vietnamese Restaurants

Typical Vietnamese restaurants have a party atmosphere and are indeed popular for special occasions. The setting is open-air with long folding tables and chairs. Menus offer a large variety of meat and seafood dishes. Vegetarian options are sparse. *Lau* (hotpot eaten family-style) is the most popular dish in these restaurants. Beer is the beverage of choice, usually served by girls in tight-fitting uniforms.

Foreign Restaurants

Foreign-owned restaurants and Vietnamese-owned restaurants serving foreign food mostly serve tourists and expats (with the exception of Chinese restaurants). The quality and variety of foreign food has vastly improved in Vietnam over the last decade, and now cuisines from France, Italy, India, Germany, the UK, the Middle East and North America are well represented. Standards range from backpacker lounges to fine, classical French dining. Some of the most notable venues include Black Cat and Sandals in Ho Chi Minh City *(see p.31, 35)*, the chains of Luna d'Autunno, Good Morning Vietnam and Shree Ganesh that are found nationwide, and Restaurant Bobby Chinn in Hanoi *(see p.81)*, with a sister restaurant just opened in Ho Chi Minh City. Service standards, atmosphere, hygiene and presentation are a much higher priority in foreign restaurants than their Vietnamese counterparts.

Fast Food and Foreign Coffee

Fast food arrived in Vietnam much later than surrounding countries. A few Western-style fast-food chains and cafes, like Lotteria (a Korean counterpart to McDonalds), Kentucky Fried Chicken and Highlands Coffee (the Vietnamese answer to Starbucks) have been around for a few years. Newer arrivals include Gloria Jean's, Coffee Bean & Tea Leaf, Pizza Hut, Popeye's and Carl's Jr. Soft-serve ice cream and donuts have also recently arrived in force, though no recognisable brands have opened yet.

DRINKS

Fruit Shakes

Vietnam cultivates a multitude of tropical fruits such as mango, custard

Water and ice

It is safest only to drink bottled water, soft drinks or boiled beverages (tea and coffee). Avoid ice in drinks on the street. Large blocks of ice are delivered each day by motorbike and laid bare on doorsteps.

apple, durian, pineapple, star fruit, rambutan and dragon fruit. Many are grown in the Mekong Delta and Da Lat, Vietnam's market garden centre. Found everywhere are *Sinh To* stalls, recognisable by their glass cases displaying a variety of fruits and a few vegetables. Point to a selection of fruit and you will receive a thick shake, mixed with sugar *(duong)*, ice and condensed milk.

Coffee and Tea

The Vietnamese love their coffee. Vietnam is the world's second-largest coffee exporter after Brazil, and domestic coffee is decent but strong. Most coffee is grown in the Central Highlands, in the vicinity of Buon Ma Thuat. Coffee *(Ca Phe)* comes iced *(da)* or hot *(nong)*; in local establishments, milk *(sua)* is usually sweetened and condensed. The Vietnamese prefer green tea, which is grown in the Central and Northern Highlands.

Wine

Grapes are grown mostly in Ninh Thuan Province, and then processed in Da Lat. Da Lat wine comes in red and white, and while palatable, it's not exciting. Thankfully, better restaurants have a large imported selection.

Rice Wine

Rice wine comes in three main varieties: plain distilled alcohol known as *ruou gao*, 'medicinal' distilled alcohol infused with plants and whole animals *(ruou thuoc)*, and *ruou can*, which is a sweet alcohol fermented in large ceramic jars by hill tribes who drink it on special occasions, through long bamboo straws.

Beer

Vietnamese are avid beer-drinkers. Saigon Beer is the popular and inexpensive local brand, with both red and green labels. Tiger and Heineken are also readily available. *Bia hoi*, or fresh (and very cheap) microbrewery beer, is particularly popular in Hanoi. The most popular branded microbreweries are the Louisiane Brewhouse in Nha Trang *(see p.49)* and the nationwide chain Hoa Vien.

Above from far left: Hue is a major Buddhist centre, so you'll have no problem finding good vegetarian dishes; Bonsai dinner cruise in HCMC; *banh xeo*, a Vietnamese crêpe.

Below: baguettes for sale – a sign of the country's former colonial ties.

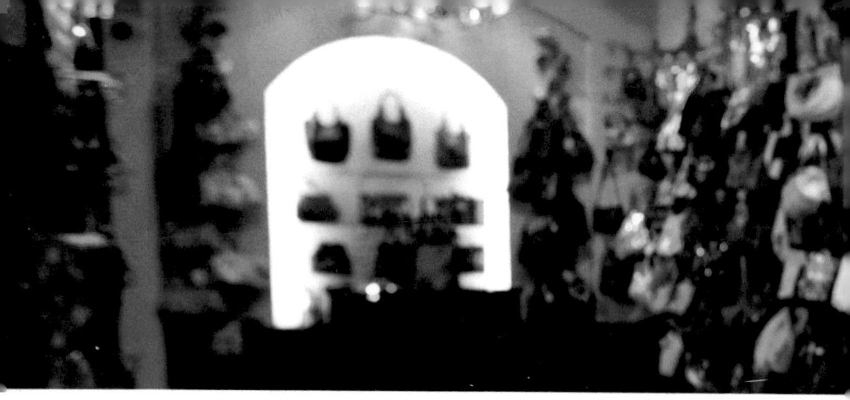

SHOPPING

Vietnam's markets are a highlight of any visit. The settings are as diverse as the goods on offer, whether paddling through Mekong floating markets, buying hill-tribe textiles right from the loom, assembling a picnic lunch from open-air markets, or procuring brand names at Saigon's high-rise malls.

Above: the clothes shop Things of Substance was set up in Hanoi by an Australian designer.

The biggest recent changes in Vietnam's shopping scene have been the creation of new, home-grown designer brands as well as a trend towards high-rise, luxury shopping malls. Stricter laws on copyright have also meant a modest reduction, but not elimination, of counterfeiting. The three main shopping destinations in Vietnam are Hanoi, Hoi An and Ho Chi Minh City.

SHOPPING AREAS

Hanoi

For those with money to burn and space in their suitcases, Hanoi can be a shopper's paradise. Exquisite silks, colourful lacquerware, gems, silver, water puppets, scarves, fake war mementoes and hand-tailored clothing can all be found at reasonable prices within the city centre. In the Old Quarter, Hang Gai (Silk Street) has a clutch of top-notch silk shops, while south on trendy Nha Tho Street, clothing, handbags and home-decor items abound. In the city's bright, air-conditioned malls, shops selling brand-name electronics, clothing and cosmetics do a booming business thanks to a new generation of affluent Vietnamese consumers.

Hoi An

Hoi An's Old Town has some of the best shopping in Vietnam. For many years Hoi An has been known as the centre of silk fabric and tailor shops, many of which are housed in the old Chinese merchant shop houses. While tailoring is key to Hoi An's economy, in recent years an increasing number of souvenir shops have joined the commercial fray. Hoi An's Central Market is located across from the Quang Cong Temple at the end of Nguyen Hue Street. You will find even better bargains on souvenirs here than at the boutique shops in town.

Ho Chi Minh City

Shopping in HCMC has dramatically improved in recent years, and it is fast emerging as a key Asian shopping and design hub. Although still a source of cheap, mass-produced goods, Vietnam's undisputed shopping capital now offers stylish, home-grown stores selling contemporary stuff at down-to-earth prices. Local

talent and HCMC-based international designers create exceptional home accessories, furniture, lighting, modern art and clothing. Many innovative designers combine ancient artisanal techniques with contemporary designs to create both decorative and practical goods.

Souvenirs like buffalo-horn servers, marble stone boxes, ceramic tea sets, silk lanterns and more are sold at the countless souvenir stores located along Dong Khoi and Le Loi streets, and around the backpacker area of De Tham and Pham Ngo Lao streets. Ben Thanh Market is the city's best-known covered market and sells piles of cheap and cheerful souvenirs and handicrafts (like lacquerware, ceramics, coffee beans, T-shirts, conical hats and more) in a relatively compact ground-floor area. At night it is also a very popular eating area, open late.

BARGAINING

Prices in Vietnam are usually negotiable, except in supermarkets where they are marked. When haggling, it is important to smile and remain polite. If a price seems high, counter-offer 50 percent and then negotiate to a happy medium. It's important not to fret too much over a few thousand dong. The difference is minimal to most foreigners, but helps locals feed their families. The most important principle in haggling is arriving at a price both parties are happy with, but not necessarily reaching the cheapest price possible.

Above: one of the two Ipa-Nima accessories shops in Hanoi.

What Not to Buy

Vietnam has very strict regulations on the sale and export of genuine antiques, and as such, most 'antique' art pieces sold to tourists are fakes or copies. If someone claims they are selling an original piece, ask to see a certificate of authenticity and ownership.

Vietnam now has strict laws prohibiting the sale of products made from endangered species and other wild animals, but there are still too many loopholes to exploit and many people who break the law outright. To be safe, don't buy insect or butterfly collections, snake wine, coral pieces, sea turtle shells, bear teeth or tiger claw necklaces. Unfortunately all are readily available, and usually come from wild, rather than captive-raised animals.

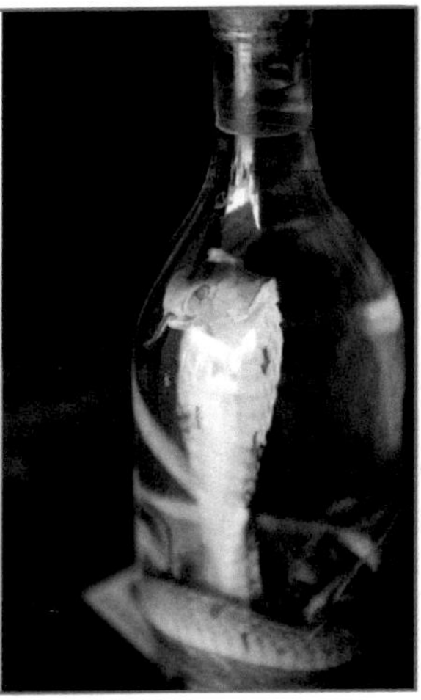

ENTERTAINMENT

Spend a night at the opera, an evening at a jazz club, or enjoy a few beers at a Saigon club. Between traditional and contemporary culture, Vietnam offers entertainment for everyone from families to young backpackers.

While certainly much more active than neighboring Cambodia or Laos, Vietnam's evening entertainment options are nonetheless a little subdued. Traditional entertainment, some of it refurbished for the tourism industry, includes water puppetry and costumed music shows. The most popular performance art throughout the country is what can best be described as classical folk opera.

Ho Chi Minh City is the centre of Vietnamese pop culture, and it is here that most of the country's pop music is produced. Likewise, all the best bars, clubs and nightlife are located here. The rest of the country is always playing catch-up with Saigon.

THEATRE

Water puppetry, though a once-popular, ancient art form, is now almost exclusively performed for tourism. While it is showcased in Ho Chi Minh City and Hue, it is most popularly scene near its place of origin, in Hanoi *(see p.87)*.

Classical folk opera comes in many names and forms, including *Cheo, Boi, Tuong* and *Cai Luong*. It is a sincere and authentic art form of rural peasants, rather than the high court. Troupes of performers travel the countryside, performing in temples and local arts centers. However some theatres, such as Cheo Hanoi Theatre *(see p.122)*, have regular shows. Unfortunately this art form appears to be dying out due to the new availability and immense popularity of cable television.

DANCE

Unlike neighbouring Cambodia, Vietnam does not have a refined classical dance tradition. Much of contemporary dance seems to have its style origins in a recycling of artless socialist propaganda rallies. There are classical ballet schools, however, which do occasionally perform at the opera houses in HCMC and Hanoi.

One exception in traditional dance is that of the Cham minority. While not as sophisticated as Thai or Khmer classical dance, it is a distinct art passed down through centuries of Hindu-influenced Cham culture. The best places to see this are in villages around the city of Phan Rang *(see p.44)*.

Stay alert
As in any country, drink responsibly while in Vietnam. Intoxicated foreign tourists are frequently the victims of fatal driving accidents, snatch-and-run robberies, sexual assault and scams.

MUSIC

Love it or hate it, it's hard to escape Vietnamese pop music. Long influenced by American music, it is beginning to become overshadowed by the influx of Korean boy-bands that have overtaken much of Southeast Asian pop culture. Vietnamese pop singers, from superstars to lounge singers, all perform at venues in big cities called *Phong Tra Ca Nhac* (Music Tea Rooms), as well as fairgrounds in the provinces.

Many bars, restaurants and hotels catering to tourists now offer live music as well. There are three categories: in-house Filipino bands which usually perform covers of oldies and contemporary pop music, classical Vietnamese court music, and, least common of the three, minor foreign rock bands who happen to be touring the country.

Jazz music has a small following in both Hanoi and HCMC. While most jazz performers get their musical training in Hanoi, the most popular spot to hear live jazz is Sax n' art *(see p.123)*, in HCMC.

FILM

There is no shortage of films about Vietnam, mostly from the American viewpoint of the war era. Notables include *The Deer Hunter* (1978), *Apocalypse Now* (1979), *Platoon* (1986), *Full Metal Jacket* (1987), *Good Morning, Vietnam* (1987), *The Scent of Green Papaya* (1993) and *The Beautiful Country* (2004). Though many travel documentaries have recently been filmed in Vietnam, few contemporary foreign films have shot in the country. The two most famous films are probably *Indochine* (1992) and *The Quiet American* (2002).

Domestic films have tended to focus on romantic comedies, Chinese mythology or revolutionary history (all, of course, pro-communist). The local film industry was neither very serious nor taken seriously until a recent influx of Vietnamese-American actors joined the industry, including Johnny Tri Nguyen *(Spider-Man 2, X-Men: First Class)* and Dustin Nguyen *(21 Jump Street, Little Fish)*. The two appeared together in the groundbreaking Vietnamese film, *The Rebel* (2007).

Since 2008 there has been an explosion of Western-style cinemas in Vietnam. The most successful brand is Megastar (www.megastar.vn), with multiple locations in HCMC, Hanoi and Da Nang.

NIGHTLIFE

Not unexpectedly, the centres of Vietnam's nightlife, in the form of popular bars and dance clubs, are HCMC and Hanoi. The best-known names include Q Bar, Le Pub and Apocalypse Now *(see p.123)*. New on the scene is Hard Rock Café *(see p.31)*, a pricey Western alternative, across from the US Consulate in HCMC.

Above from far left: water puppet show; Vine wine bar in Hanoi.

Above: on the decks and at the bar in Hanoi's Funky Buddha.

FESTIVALS

At times Vietnamese culture can look like one party after another. Whether it's the Lunar New Year, the Mid-Autumn Festival or Buddha's Birthday, there's a festival – or several festivals – to celebrate every month.

Vietnam has a vast number of traditional religious and cultural festivals. Some are celebrated across the country, but each province, and often each village or temple, may have its own unique calendar of events. All traditional festivals occur according to the lunar calendar (a gift from the Chinese); a few dates may be altered according to messages from sacred oracles (or the local 'People's Committee' governing board).

Common elements in traditional festivals include temple visits, offerings to ancestors or tutelary gods, costumes, dragon and lion dancing, music, parades and lots of food.

January–February

Tet (first–third day of first lunar month). The biggest and most important celebration of the entire year, Tet Nguyen Dan (in full) heralds the start of the Vietnamese Lunar New Year. The most important days of Tet ('festival') are the first three days of the Lunar New Year. However, the holiday ceremonially lasts for two weeks. Either way the whole country shuts down for about a week. Everyone returns home for the holidays, including many overseas Vietnamese. The most interesting time for visitors is actually the week prior to the holiday, when night markets are a commotion of candy, flower and lantern vendors. Tet eve is celebrated with fireworks and dragon and lion dancing.

Hai Ba Trung Festival (sixth day of the second lunar month). This festival is held in Hanoi, at the Hai Ba Trung Temple. It honours the heroic resistance of the Trung sisters against the Chinese.

March–April

Perfume Pagoda Festival (15th day of the second lunar month). Thousands of Buddhist pilgrims flock to one of Vietnam's most revered pilgrimage sites, southwest of Hanoi *(see tour 14)*, to pray for good luck in the coming year.

Holiday of the Dead (fifth day of the third lunar month). On this day many people visit the graves of their ancestors to tend them and make offerings.

Elephant Race Festival (middle of the third lunar month). Elephant races occur in Ban Don Village near Buon Ma Thuat, and they are a traditional event for the M'Nong tribe. Ethnic music, dancing and drinking of *ruou can* (bamboo pole wine) are all part of the festivities.

Public holidays

1 Jan: New Year's Day
Jan/Feb: Tet
3 Feb: Founding of Vietnamese Communist Party
10th day of the third lunar month: Hung Kings Day
30 Apr: Liberation Day
1 May: International Labour Day
19 May: Ho Chi Minh's Birthday
June: Buddha's Birthday (eighth day of the fourth lunar month)
2 Sept: National Day/ Independence Day

Thay Pagoda Festival (fifth–seventh day of the third lunar month). In celebration of the pagoda's revered Buddhist monk and puppeteer, the festivities include water puppetry and rowing contests.

May–June

Phat Dan (eighth day of the fourth lunar month). Buddha's rites of passage are celebrated in pagodas, temples and homes, and sometimes with parades.

Tet Doan Ngo (Summer Solstice Day; fifth day of the fifth lunar month). This Tet includes festivities to ensure good health and well-being. Offerings are made to spirits, ghosts and the God of Death, to ward off summer epidemics.

Trang Nguyen (Wandering Souls Day; 15th day of the seventh lunar month). This is the second-most important Vietnamese festival. Graves are cleaned and offerings are made for the wandering souls of the forgotten dead.

Hue City Festival. This is a biennial celebration during even-numbered years, celebrating the Nguyen Dynasty and the cultural heritage of Hue. Expect parades, lots of performers, games and numerous special events.

September–October

Tet Trung Thu (Mid-Autumn Festival; 15th day of the eighth lunar month). Children parade around with candle-illuminated lanterns, and delicious pastry-covered 'mooncakes' with sweet lotus-seed or red-bean paste are eaten.

Kate Festival (eighth or ninth lunar month). Getting the date right of this Cham festival (often mistakenly called the 'Cham New Year') is difficult because it falls within a unique Cham lunar calendar. It's usually early October. The festival is held at ancient Cham temples in Phan Thiet and Phan Rang, with feasting, music and processions.

Whale Festival (16th–18th day of the eighth lunar month). Known as both Lang Ca Ong and Cau Ngu, it is celebrated in Vung Tau and other southern fishing communities. In Phan Thiet it occurs in odd-numbered years. Festivities include parades with costumed performers, dragon and lion dances, and processions of whale bones.

November–December

Da Lat Flower Festival. This is a week-long festival with parades, street food, games, live music, and endless flower markets and flower exhibits. Occasionally it may occur in January.

Above from far left: leaving offerings at Tay Ho Pagoda; Buddhist monks at Phuoc Lam Pagoda in Hoi An.

Below: Liberation Day marks the surrender of South Vietnam to the North Vietnamese Army in 1975.

HISTORY: KEY DATES

Wars, wars and more wars... Despite a violent history of conflict for more than 1,000 years with the Chinese, Cham, French, Japanese, Cambodians and Americans, Vietnam's rich culture has flourished and evolved into an exceedingly diverse, but fairly unified nation.

CHINA AND THE STRUGGLE FOR INDEPENDENCE

258BC Thuc Pan establishes new Vietnamese state called Au Lac.
207BC Trieu Da, renegade Chinese general, conquers Au Lac and establishes power over Nam Viet.
111BC Heirs of Trieu Da submit to Han Chinese emperor.
AD40 Trung sisters lead first major rebellion against Chinese.
938 Ngo Quyen wins Bach Dang battle, ending 1,000 years of Chinese rule.
1516 Portuguese seafarers are first Westerners to arrive in Vietnam.
1539–1778 Trinh lords rule north, while Nguyen lords control south.

THE NGUYEN DYNASTY AND THE FRENCH

1802–19 Nguyen Anh defeats Tay Sons, proclaiming himself Emperor Gia Long, establishing the Nguyen Dynasty.
1820–40 Emperor Minh Mang hostile to Christianity during his reign.
1861 French forces capture Saigon.
1862 Tu Duc signs a compromising peace treaty with the French.
1883 France establishes protectorate, ruling Cochinchina as a colony.

COMMUNISM AND REBELLION

1890 Birth of Ho Chi Minh.
1930 Ho forms Vietnamese Communist Party.
1940 Japan occupies Vietnam, leaving French administration intact.
1945 Japan defeated; Ho Chi Minh declares independence and Vietnam a Democratic Republic.
1946 French bombard Haiphong. Viet Minh withdraws from Hanoi. First Indochina War begins.
1954 Battle of Dien Bien Phu. Geneva Accord divides Vietnam: south led by Catholic Ngo Dinh Diem, north by communist Ho Chi Minh.

Progression?
Since 2008, Vietnam appears to have been going in two directions. While economic progress rapidly speeds ahead, Vietnam has begun reining in freedoms of religion, speech and the press.

WAR WITH AMERICA

1955 Diem refuses to hold general elections. Second Indochina War begins.
1960 North Vietnam introduces conscription. First US advisers in South.
1965 US President Johnson commences bombing of North; first US combat troops land at Danang.
1968 US troops rise to 540,000, but Tet Offensive saps morale.
1969 Ho Chi Minh dies aged 79; US begins phased withdrawal of troops.
1973 Washington and Hanoi sign ceasefire. Last US troops withdrawn.

REUNIFICATION

1975 NVA captures Saigon. Vietnam unified. US imposes trade embargo.
1976 Socialist Republic of Vietnam declared.
1978 Cambodian troops mount cross-border attacks into southern Vietnam. Vietnam invades Cambodia, overthrowing Khmer Rouge.
1979 China retaliates by invading northern Vietnam.

MODERNISATION

1986 6th Party Congress embraces Doi Moi (economic renovation).
1991 China relations normalised.
1993 Restrictions on Vietnam borrowing from IMF are lifted.
1994 US Trade Embargo lifted.
1995 Vietnam becomes official member of ASEAN (Association of Southeast Asian Nations).
2000 Bill Clinton becomes first US president to visit since the war.
2001 US–Vietnam Bilateral Trade Agreement signed.
2003 Vietnam hosts 22nd SEA Games.
2004 Hill Tribes Protest in Central Highlands, government cracks down.
2006 APEC summit held in Hanoi.
2007 Vietnam joins World Trade Organization (WTO).
2008 Government jails journalists who covered 2006 'PMU 18' corruption scandal.
2009 Chinese government mines bauxite in Central Highlands, igniting protests.
2010 US publicly sides with Vietnam against China in territorial dispute.

Above: the War Remnants Museum in HCMC is a must-visit for those with an interest in the Vietnam War with America.

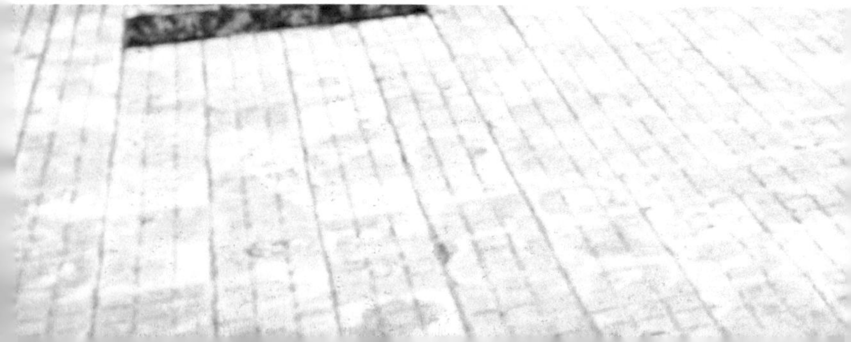

WALKS AND TOURS

HO CHI MINH CITY: THE QUIET AMERICAN IN THE 21ST CENTURY

Relive Graham Greene's famous novel The Quiet American, *right where he wrote it. However, modern Ho Chi Minh City is not 1950s Saigon; soak up the contrast of old and new in Vietnam's flashy economic capital.*

DISTANCE 5.7km (3½ miles)
TIME A full-day walk through bustling city
START Hotel Majestic
END Former American Legation at intersection of Ham Nghi and Ho Tung Mau streets
POINTS TO NOTE
This tour can easily be merged with tour 2, as streets overlap. Transport by taxi and motorbike is available, as well as cyclo (though the latter not recommended for safety).

Read *The Quiet American* before setting out. In the 1955 novel, Graham Greene's Fowler attempts to lay bare the bones of one of Saigon's most Machiavellian eras. Set in the twilight of French influence, the novel recalls a murky 'what might have been' scenario tracing the outset of US involvement in Vietnam. Greene's Saigon is filled with war correspondents, doomed innocents and glasses of vermouth cassis.

Changing Cholon

During colonial times, Cholon (Saigon's Chinatown) was a dangerous area, rife with gangsters and communist revolutionaries. Some, though, found it a glamorous, fascinating place; Greene spent time here, allegedly sampling the opium dens. Today it is an atmospheric blend of ancient Chinese temples, bustling markets and the new Hung Vuong Shopping Centre and Megastar Cineplex.

THE RIVERFRONT

Begin at the **Hotel Majestic** ❶ (1 Dong Khoi Street). Built by the French in 1925, this was one of Southeast Asia's classic colonial hotels. The rooftop bar commands great views of the **Saigon River**. In the 1950s, covering the Franco-Viet Minh War, British war correspondent Graham Greene lived in Suite R404, where he wrote some of *The Quiet American.*

To your right lies the **Port of Saigon**, the largest port in Vietnam. The big salmon-pink building on the opposite side of the river is the old customs house, nicknamed 'Dragon House', and built by a French mercantile company in 1862. It was from here that Ho Chi Minh set off on his 30 years of travels.

DONG KHOI STREET

Turn left out of the Majestic and walk up **Dong Khoi Street** away from the river. In the early 1900s, this tree-lined boulevard was known as Rue Catinat, edged with fashionable boutiques,

cafés and theatres. The epicentre of the original French Quarter, the impressive edifices built along here by the colonials are today some of the city's key historical sights.

Dong Khoi is now the city's main tourism and commercial street, lined with fashionable boutiques, art galleries, souvenir shops, shopping plazas and five-star hotels. It offers broad choices in merchandise, including hill-tribe crafts, silk, lacquer and oil paintings, as well as imported brands like Calvin Klein, Gucci, Louis Vuitton and Versace.

Bisecting Dong Khoi is **Mac Thi Buoi Street**, previously Rue d'Ormay. This street housed one of the notorious opium dens that Greene's protagonist, Fowler, was so fond of. Today it also has many interesting boutiques.

LAM SON SQUARE

Continuing up Dong Khoi, you'll arrive at Lam Son Square, at the corner of Dong Khoi Street and Le Loi Boulevard. Formerly Place Garnier, this was the setting of General Thé's terrorist bombing in *The Quiet American*. Opposite on Dong Khoi was the Girval Café, where Greene's Phuong stopped for her 'elevenses', or for afternoon tea. The entire block is now under renovation for a new shopping centre.

On the northern side of the square, the colonial **Hotel Continental** ❷ no longer has the famous Continental Shelf Café, where Fowler sipped vermouth cassis. However, it retains the charming inner courtyard café. Graham Greene wrote much of *The Quiet American* here, while residing in Room 214.

Above from far left: skyline of HCMC; urban fashion for men and women at Mai's on Dong Khoi.

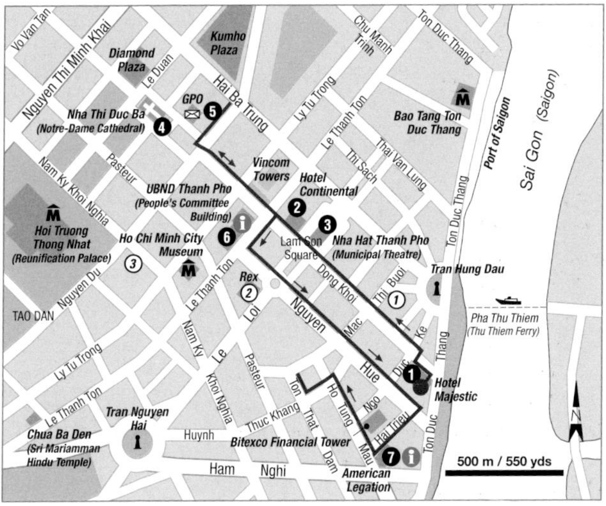

What's in a name?
With France's departure in 1954, Rue Catinat was renamed Tu Do (Freedom Street) and during the Vietnam War degenerated into a sleazy street lined with raucous bars and clubs. Following the South's 'liberation' in 1975, the street was renamed Dong Khoi (Popular Uprising).

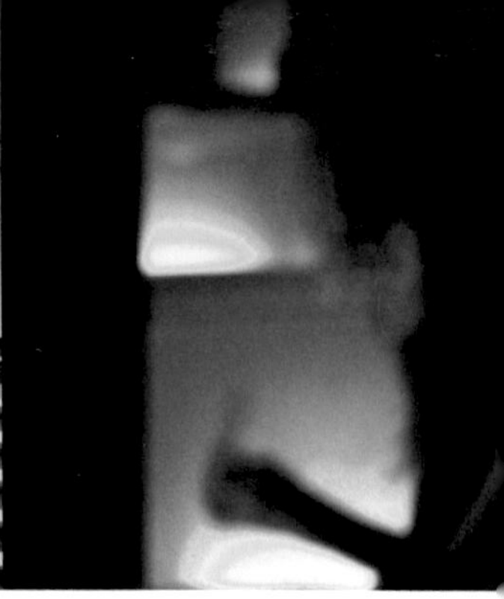

The neoclassical **Municipal Theatre** ❸ (Nha Hat Thanh Pho) stands sandwiched between the Continental, Park Hyatt Saigon and towering Caravelle Hotel. This former opera house hosts occasional classical music and dance performances, advertised by banners outside.

At this point a diversion to **Black Cat**, see 🍴①, is in order for lunch. Backtrack two blocks on Dong Khoi, turn left to the northeast, then right on Phan Van Dat.

NOTRE-DAME CATHEDRAL AND POST OFFICE

Continuing up Dong Khoi Street, you'll pass the sparkling **Vincom Towers**. This enormous shopping plaza is the largest in Vietnam and since 2010 has housed Carl's Jr, the first American fast-food burger chain to arrive in the country.

Straight ahead is **Notre-Dame Cathedral** ❹ (Nha Thi Duc Ba), described by Graham Greene as 'the hideous pink Cathedral' in the aftermath of the bombing at Place Garnier. Inaugurated in 1880, it was designed to mirror Notre-Dame de Paris. Mass is conducted at 5.30am and 5pm daily, with seven services on Sunday. Other visiting times are restricted (Mon–Sat 8–10.30am and 3–4pm).

The salmon-hued building to the right is the **General Post Office** ❺ (daily 7am–8pm), another impressive colonial-era edifice. Behind it on Hai

The Cao Dai Holy See

In the 1920s, Ngo Van Chieu formed the Cao Dai religion, following a revelation of 'The Way' in a dream. In 1926, one of his followers, Le Van Trung, deserted with 20,000 disciples, crowned himself pontiff and built the Cao Dai Temple at Tay Ninh, north of Saigon. Graham Greene described the temple as 'a Walt Disney fantasia of the East'. Seven years later, Le Van Trung was deposed for embezzling the temple funds.

Cao Daism seeks to create the ultimate religion by fusing Buddhist, Taoist, Confucian and Catholic beliefs into a synthesis of its own. Today, around 3 million Vietnamese still follow the Cao Dai Way, although sermons by planchette–séances – which used to be held to contact 'saints' like Sun Yat Sen and Victor Hugo – are no longer practised. Tourists flock to the bizarre cathedral, and the 'joke gone too far' (according to Greene) seems set to remain.

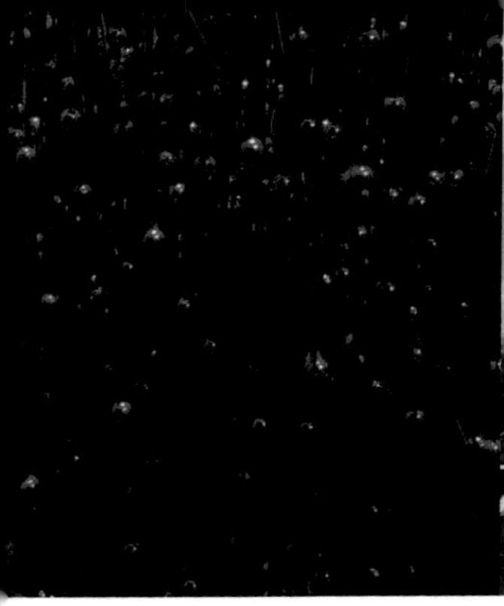

Ba Trung Street is the **Hard Rock Café Saigon**, another 2010 arrival.

NGUYEN HUE AND HAM NHI STREETS

Head back to Lam Son Square and look to the northern end of Nguyen Hue Street for the lavish **People's Committee Building** ❻ (UBND Thanh Pho). Formerly the French administrative headquarters, this is one of the city's loveliest landmarks. An imposing statue of Ho Chi Minh stands in front.

Turn into **Nguyen Hue Street**, formerly Boulevard Charner and today an eclectic jumble of old and new architecture. Note the old bank building at No. 37 on your right as you head towards the river. The facade, in charming colonial style, has been retained, while modern high-rises tower behind.

Turn right into Hai Trieu and continue until you reach the former **American Legation** ❼, on the corner of Ham Nghi and Ho Tung Mau streets. Now a bank, this striking 1950s block was where the character Pyle conducted his nefarious affairs close to Mr Muoi's bomb factory. On the other side of Ho Tung Mau is the new **Bitexco Financial Tower**. At 68 storeys, it is currently the tallest building in Vietnam, complete with its own helicopter pad. It has recently opened an elevator ride to the top of the building (ticket price $10), where tourists can get a 360-degree panorama of the city and take photos to their heart's content. The views are spectacular on a sunny day.

Further up on the right, **Ton That Dam Street** was originally the location of 'Thieves' Market', where all manner of second-hand goods used to end up. Now this neighbourhood is a centre for Saigon's trade in pirated DVDs, digital music and electronics.

Round the day off with a cocktail at the **Rex Rooftop Garden Bar**, see ②, at the Rex Hotel, overlooking The People's Committee Building. Then sample authentic, inexpensive Vietnamese street food at **Quan An Ngon**, see ③, on Nam Ky Khoi Nghia Street, just two blocks south down Le Loi.

Above from far left: Municipal Theatre; HCMC's glamourous nightlife scene; the People's Committee Building.

Food and Drink

① BLACK CAT
13 Phan Van Dat Street; tel: 08-3829 2055; daily B, L & D; $$$
Recognised by CNN as offering one of the best burgers in the world, Black Cat is a sanctuary of Western comfort food. The menu includes pizza, Indian and their famous fruit shakes utilising local and hard-to-find imported fruits and sorbets.

② REX ROOFTOP GARDEN BAR
Rex Hotel, 141 Nguyen Hue Street; tel: 08-3829 2185; daily D; $$$
The fifth-floor open terrace offers bird's-eye views of downtown, and its giant crown, illuminated at night, is one of the city's best-known landmarks. The historic bar is a favourite of expats and visitors alike.

③ QUAN AN NGON
138 Nam Ky Khoi Nghia Street; tel: 08-3825 7179; daily D; $$
Quang An Ngon is popular with both local Vietnamese and expats. At around 5pm folding tables and chairs roll out onto the sidewalk to create a temporary smorgasbord of Vietnamese seafood and popular cuisine with ice-cold beer.

2

HO CHI MINH CITY: WAR REMNANTS

This one-day walking tour takes you through Old Saigon's downtown District 1 and gives a glimpse into the former capital's wartime past through museums, shopping for war memorabilia and an atmospheric stroll.

DISTANCE A 4km (2½-mile) walk
TIME A full day
START Reunification Palace
END Antique Shops at Le Cong Kieu Street
POINTS TO NOTE
This is a relatively comfortable walking tour through downtown Ho Chi Minh City. It can be intermingled with tour 1 too. Be mindful of valuables while walking on the street, as snatch-and-run thievery is on the increase in this area.

Stay safe
Do not go away with anyone who casually approaches you on the street in Saigon and invites you for coffee or to their home to meet their family. A Filipino mafia stalks tourists at attractions in this part of the city. Victims lose thousands of dollars every day.

On 30 April 1975, the camera that had focused on South Vietnam for decades was abruptly blanked out. The final images seen in the West were those of the fall of the South Vietnamese capital, Saigon: the roof of the US Embassy where the last departing helicopter was battling with crowds scrambling for space, and tanks storming through the Presidential Palace. What followed were 15 years of deprivation and austerity as the victorious Northerners imposed their land reform and free trade restrictions on the Southerners.

Since the 1990s, however, Ho Chi Minh City (Thanh Pho Ho Chi Minh) has risen, phoenix-like, from the ashes of former Saigon. This sprawling mass of humanity is Vietnam's commercial and economic hub, and the nation's largest and most populated city.

REUNIFICATION PALACE

Take a taxi or walk to the **Reunification Palace** ❶ (Hoi Truong Thong Nhat; tel: 08-3822 3652; daily 7.30–11am, 1–4pm; charge) at the junction of Nam Ky Khoi Nghia Street and Le Duan Boulevard. It was formerly known as the Presidential Palace and headquarters of the Government of South Vietnam; work on the edifice started shortly before President Diem's assassination in 1963. By then, his helicopter pad, dance floor and cinema had already been planned. The architect, Ngo Viet Thu, a 1960s purist, designed details from chandeliers to carpets specifically for

the palace, making it one of the few totally contemporary state buildings of this era.

Inside the entrance are poster-size photographs of the 1970s. One of these is the famous image taken by NBC's Neil Davies of a Russian tank forcing down the palace gates on 30 April 1975, spelling the demise of South Vietnam and its government. General Duong Van Minh, South Vietnam's president for just 24 hours, surrendered to the Northern forces minutes later.

The optional guided tour takes in several floors, including the cabinet meeting room, president's private residential quarters and cinema, plus bomb-proof basement, containing Nguyen Van Thieu's (president 1967–75) war operations rooms, complete with original war maps.

WAR REMNANTS MUSEUM

Walk north up Nam Ky Khoi Nghia Street to Vo Van Tan Street and turn left to find at No. 28 the **War Remnants Museum** ❷ (Bao Tang Chung Tich Chien Tranh; 28 Vo Van Tan Street; tel: 08-3930 2112; daily 7.30am–noon, 1.30–5pm; charge), set in the former headquarters of the US Information Services. You need a strong stomach as the museum comes to grips with the nastier aspects of Vietnam's recent history, such as human embryos in jars and pictures of deformed children, depicting the effectiveness of the defoliant Agent Orange, gory photographs of war mutilations and a guillotine used for decapitating agitators in the 1920s riots. One of the exhibition halls, entitled **Requiem**, holds works of photographers from many countries who died in war conflicts in Indochina. Outside in the forecourt, there is an impressive array of military hardware, including tanks, a helicopter and a fighter jet.

Above from far left: Reunification Palace; War Remnants Museum.

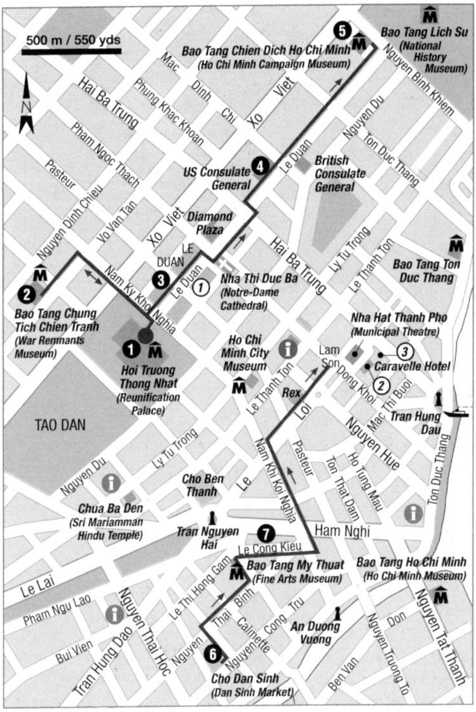

Although a visit here is likely to be distressing, it is a sobering reminder of the heavy toll of war.

LE DUAN BOULEVARD AND CONSULATES

Backtrack towards the Reunification Palace. The gardens bordering the Palace and Le Duan Boulevard were once the palace gardens; now known as **Le Duan Park** ❸, this small oasis is edged by cafés. Le Duan was previously Norodom Boulevard, which developed as a diplomatic and residential enclave with pastel-hued colonial villas. A fine example still standing is the **French Consulate General**, at No. 6, the only Western delegation to remain open throughout 1975 and afterwards. Heading eastwards along Le Duan, the next building on your left is the **US Consulate General** ❹, constructed over the original embassy building. In 1968, millions of television viewers watched agape as a Viet Cong special forces broke into the embassy grounds during the Tet Offensive. The original building had another, greater, starring role when the last US helicopter left from its grounds in 1975, carrying a man aloft on a rope just seconds after the US Ambassador swept his country's flag away in ignominy and stepped into the helicopter. The new US Consulate General, built after the half-derelict embassy was demolished in 1999, signifies a new era in US–Vietnamese relations. Diagonally across the road at No. 25 is the former British Embassy, now the **British Consulate General**.

Cu Chi Tunnels

Located about 70km (44 miles) to the northwest of HCMC, the Cu Chi Tunnels are one of Vietnam's proudest patriotic shrines and achievements during the Vietnam War. From these hiding places, Viet Cong were able to spring devastating surprise attacks on their enemies. In fact, by the mid-1960s, it is believed that over 200km (124 miles) of tunnels laced the region around Cu Chi. The tunnels ran up to 10m (33ft) deep, each with a breadth of between 0.5 to 1m (1½ to 3ft), and stacked up to three levels. The top tier could support the weight of a 50-tonne tank, while the middle layer could withstand moderate mortar attacks. The lowest level was virtually impregnable. Located at the end of the Ho Chi Minh Trail, and straddling both Highway 1 and the Saigon River, the tunnels were of vital strategic importance. However, some of the government's claims about the comfort and technological advances of the tunnels are unlikely.

HO CHI MINH MUSEUM

At the eastern end of Le Duan, at No. 2, the **Ho Chi Minh Campaign Museum** ❺ (Bao Tang Chien Dich Ho Chi Minh; tel: 08-3822 9387; Sun, Tue–Fri 8–11.30am and Sun, Tue–Thur 1.30–4.30pm; charge) is devoted to recording the campaign by North Vietnamese communist troops as they captured the south in 1974–5.

For lunch, head back to Le Duan Park for lunch at **Au Parc**, see ①, on Han Thuyen Street.

WAR MEMORABILIA-SHOPPING

After lunch, take a taxi to **Dan Sinh Market** ❻ (Cho Dan Sinh), on the corner of Yersin and Nguyen Cong Tru streets. Also known as 'Yersin Market' or the 'War Surplus Market', it is slowly being dismantled, but stalls still sell a vast jumble of armed forces clothing, goods and wartime memorabilia. While a little stock is genuine vintage, most is new surplus or mass-produced reproduction and includes US Army hard helmets, GI dog tags and inscribed Zippo lighters.

Two blocks northeast, opposite the Fine Arts Museum, **Le Cong Kieu Street** ❼ has long been known as 'Antique Street'. Along this atmospheric small stretch, the row of narrow, open-fronted dwellings are devoted to sales of oriental and colonial bric-a-brac, furniture and decor, either reproduction or vintage.

Heading north, turn left on Nam Khi Koi Nghia Street and then take a right on Le Loi Street. **Caravelle Hotel**, at Lam Son Square (in front of the Municipal Theatre) has a perfect place for a pre-dinner cocktail at its **Saigon Saigon Bar**, see ②. Follow up with dinner just around the corner at **Sandals,** see ③.

Food and Drink

① AU PARC

23 Han Thuyen Street; tel: 08-3829 2772; daily B, L & D; $$$

Deco tile floors and high ceilings give Au Parc a distinctly French ambience. A choice of excellent baguette sandwiches, in addition to a variety of Mediterranean plates and *mezze,* are available indoors on one of several air-conditioned floors or outside on the patio, overlooking Le Duan Park.

② SAIGON SAIGON BAR

Caravelle Hotel, 19 Lam Son Square; tel: 08-3823 4999; daily L & D; $$$

This rooftop bar not only boasts one of the best downtown views from the 10th-floor, but during the Vietnam War it was home to numerous American press corps and became an infamous 'centre of operations' for many war correspondents. Stop here for a cocktail and to soak up the city vistas.

③ SANDALS RESTAURANT AND BAR

93 Hai Ba Trung Street; tel: 08-3827 5198; daily L & D; $$$$

Part of the Sailing Club empire in Vietnam, Sandals provides intimate and elegant dining in an oasis among the clamour and hustle of downtown Saigon. The menu puts seafood and Vietnamese fusion front and centre, with Middle Eastern highlights.

Above from far left: the Fine Arts Museum; portrait of Uncle Ho using buttons and sequins, HCM Campaign Museum; stall at Dan Sinh Market.

Antique-hunting

Antique experts say that 70–90 percent of the antiques on Le Cong Kieu Street are reproductions. There are, however, some hidden treasures, including rare ancient relics from the Champa, Sa Huynh, Funan and Dong Son cultures. Be advised that antiques must be accompanied with a certificate to exit the country.

3

THE MEKONG DELTA

This three-day trip to Vinh Long and Can Tho, in the heart of the Mekong Delta, lets you peek into the romantic ambience of the region. Meander through small waterways to floating markets and island gardens, and relax in munificent fruit orchards.

DISTANCE Day 1: 140km (87 miles); Day 2: 246km (153 miles)
TIME 3 days
START/END Ho Chi Minh City
POINTS TO NOTE
Hire a car or motorcycle from the backpacker area in Ho Chi Minh City around De Tham and Pham Ngu Lao streets. Alternatively, a country bus ticket can be purchased at the bus station at the northern terminus of Pham Ngu Lao Street, in front of Ben Thanh Market. Plan to leave Ho Chi Minh City in the afternoon for the 138km (86-mile), three-hour journey, so that you arrive in Vinh Long in time to catch the sunset. For accommodation choices, see the Directory, p.114.

There are many viable options for routes between HCMC and the cities in this tour, so be sure to bring a map. This tour is suitable for the whole family and is more about soaking up the landscape and ambience than visiting landmarks.

The Mekong River flows over 4,500km (2,800 miles) from the frozen wastes of Tibet through China, Laos, Cambodia and finally Vietnam before emptying into the sea. The nine provinces of the Delta area, beginning at Tan An, 40km (25 miles) from HCMC, are known as Cuu Long, or Nine Dragons, in reference to the nine tributaries of the Mekong. The number 9 is considered lucky in Vietnamese geomancy, and the Mekong Delta has certainly been lucky for its inhabitants. Silt from the Himalayan Plateau has made this area Vietnam's rice bowl. The delta is prone to extensive flooding, sometimes with serious consequences. During the rainy season months of May to November, some roads are impassable.

Khmer history
The Mekong Delta once belonged exclusively to the Khmers. The ancient archaeological site of Oc Eo, located in An Giang Province, was an important port city of the pre-Angkorian Funan Empire. Vietnam, however, downplays this history due to ethnic and political tensions.

VINH LONG

Vinh Long ❶ is 34km (21 miles) from the municipality of Can Tho, the region's economic centre, and 70km (43 miles) from industrial My Tho. This provincial capital (the province is also named Vinh Long) sprawls along the southern shore of the Tien Giang, or Upper Mekong River. Although a city,

Vinh Long is typical of this region: small, friendly and without a bustling centre. There are a few architectural remnants from French colonial times, a market and a handful of hotels, but, as with this entire region, the main action is on and around the river.

In Vinh Long, secure a boat, either for the next day or to take you to your guesthouse on Binh Hoa Phuoc Island, if you have booked a homestay. For the latter, contact **Cuu Long Tourist** (tel: 070-382 3616; www.cuulongtourist.com), located on the ground floor of Cuu Long B Hotel at Number 1, 1 Thang 5 Street. Boats from Cuu Long Tourist are fairly expensive, but its English-speaking guides are well informed and can explain some of the area's mysteries to you. Alternatively, go to the An Binh Boat Station and negotiate.

Then settle back and enjoy the sunset over the Tien Giang River from the **Phuong Thuy Restaurant**, see 🍴①, located just across from the Cuu Long B Hotel.

Cai Be Floating Market

The next morning, meet your boatman for the three-hour return ride to **Cai Be Floating Market** ❷ (daily 5am–5pm). This is a good place to eat breakfast or to buy a picnic lunch. Fresh produce, hand-woven baskets, palm sugar, buffalo horn and coconut utensils and a myriad of other goods are all on offer.

As you leave the dock, you will see people all along the riverbank tending

Food and Drink

① PHUONG THUY RESTAURANT

1, 1 Thang 5; tel: 070-382 4786; daily B, L & D; $$$

Phuong Thuy is a traditional Vietnamese restaurant offering great views of the Tien Giang River. The staff are friendly and helpful, even if their English isn't spot-on. Happily, it has an English-language menu and offers favourites like spring rolls (*cha gio*), fresh seafood, stir-fried noodles, fried rice, and caramelised pork in a clay pot.

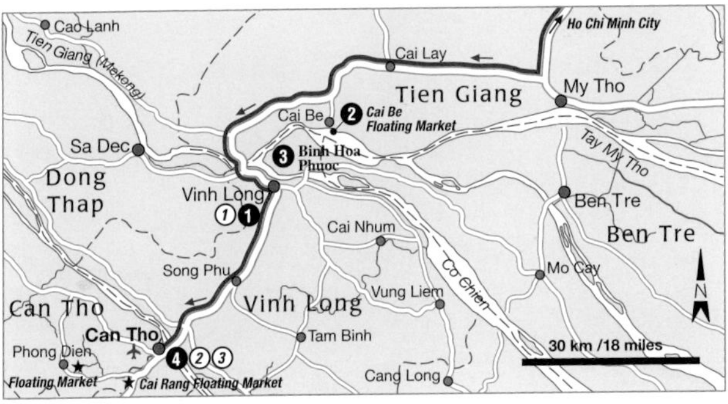

Above from far left: Van Thanh Mieu temple in Vinh Long; Cai Rang floating market near Can Tho.

to their household chores or washing (women bathe with all their clothes on) and children playing in the water. Many families have small sampans. Look out for the ones with great eyes painted red and black on their prows: these are ocean-going vessels, painted so they can see their way safely to the sea. You will see rice barges filled with seasonal, tropical fruits such as bananas, mangosteens and Java apples. Rice, fish and flowers are also traded from boats at the floating market. Along the shoreline, fish traps spear the water.

Binh Toa Phuoc Island

Head for **Nguyen Thanh Giao's (Ong Giao) House** in **Binh Hoa Phuoc ❸**, east of Vinh Long. The garden, filled with numerous bonsai trees, is an idyllic spot for a rest in a hammock with a book, and it is even better for lunch.

Study your map for other gardens and orchards to visit on An Binh and Binh Hoa Phuoc islands (or ask the boatman to recommend some). This is where a guide will help if you are interested in seeing how tropical fruits are grown. Rambutans, longans – the most

Bridges and Ferries

After a 2½-hour drive from HCMC, you'll reach a suspension bridge just before Vinh Long. Previously the water was dotted with ferries. These huge clanking rafts carried everything from the school bus to street vendors and weather-beaten farmers. Only Ben Tre Province, Chau Doc City and a few minor roads are served by these lumbering machines today. The crossings are only a few minutes and will throw anyone enraptured by the film *The Lover* into a romantic reverie.

Ferries have always been an essential part of life in the Mekong, which is prone to seasonal flooding. Some roads and many villages are inaccessible by road in the rainy season. They range from large wooden canoes with motors, which may carry people, livestock, merchant goods and motorbikes or farm equipment, to massive barges transporting cars, buses and trucks.

important fruit in this area – mangoes and pineapples all produce abundant crops in the Mekong Delta's rich soil.

Elephant ear fish *(ca tai tuong)*, the local speciality, is as large as a soup plate and delicately flavoured. Sample some while you are on the island, wrapped in rice paper with salad, then dipped in a sauce.

CAN THO

In the evening travel 45 minutes' drive and 34km (21 miles) southwest of Vinh Long to the major ferry centre of **Can Tho** ❹, the largest town and effective capital of the Mekong Delta. Here the presence of Vietnam's substantial Khmer Krom community begins to make itself felt. **Munirangsyaram Pagoda** at 36 Hoa Binh Street, for example, is a Therevada Buddhist temple very similar to those in Cambodia; minus the Bodhisattvas and Taoist spirits found in Vietnamese Mahayana temples.

Can Tho is a good place to stay overnight, as the accommodation available is the best in the delta, and good restaurants are aplenty. For food, head to **Nam Bo**, see ②, at 50 Hai Ba Trung along the waterfront, for excellent seafood.

Floating Markets

It's a good idea to rise early and take a boat trip to see one of the local floating markets; but note that business slows down by 8.30am. There are two worthwhile floating markets near Can Tho: **Cai Rang** is about 5km (3 miles) southeast of the city centre, while **Phong Dien** lies about 20km (12 miles) to the southwest. If you're feeling energetic, Phong Dien is the better bet as it is less crowded.

After your watery shopping adventure, return to Can Tho for a leisurely lunch at **Spices**, see ③, in the Victoria Can Tho Hotel, and enjoy the river views. Don't stay too late, as it takes around three hours to drive back to Ho Chi Minh City.

Food and Drink

② NAM BO

50 Hai Ba Trung; tel: 0710-382 3908; daily B, L & D; $$$

Nam Bo is set in a lovely French colonial villa along the waterfront and surrounded by gardens. Seating is indoors or on the upstairs terrace. The menu includes traditional Vietnamese and seafood as well as Western standards like pizza, soups, salads, sandwiches and pasta.

③ SPICES

Victoria Can Tho Hotel, Cai Khe Ward; tel: 0710-381 0111; daily B, L & D; $$$$

Seating at the featured restaurant of the Victoria Hotel is indoors or outside on the riverside terrace. The menu includes traditional Vietnamese and seafood, fine French, Italian and an American-style buffet. The restaurant is elegantly decorated in a Mekong theme, and service is excellent.

Above from far left: trader at Cai Rang market; exhibit at Can Tho Museum; making incense.

The Cham

Besides the Khmers and Chinese (or Hoa), the Cham are the other common minority in the Mekong. Cham Bani practise an ancient form of Islam blended with indigenous traditions of their cousins, the Cham Balamon of Binh Thuan and Ninh Thuan Province. Cham Islam is more recent, with influence from communities in Malaysia, Indonesia and the Middle East.

4

PANDURANGA

Frolic in Mui Ne, Vietnam's most popular beach resort, before taking an epic journey through desert landscapes, exploring some of the oldest monuments of the Champa Kingdom, in the modern homeland of the Cham people.

DISTANCE Day 1: 150km (93 miles); Day 2: 50km (31 miles)
TIME 2 days
START Thap Po Shanu (Cham Temple in Phan Thiet)
END Thap Po Klong Garai (Cham Temple in Phan Rang)
POINTS TO NOTE
This tour is best used as a bridge between Ho Chi Minh City and Nha Trang. Phan Thiet (Mui Ne) is accessible from HCMC by train and bus. Travel on this tour is best by car or motorbike with a knowledgeable guide. Recommendations include Jaka (tel: 091-917 4987; inrajaka@yahoo.com) in Phan Rang/Ninh Thuan Province or Hung (tel: 090-443 4895; info@muinebeach.net) for Binh Thuan Province.

Mui Ne
Before you begin this tour, be sure to spend some time at one of Mui Ne's resorts. Also, take an evening to enjoy the live Cham music, dancing and weaving demonstrations at the Forest Restaurant.

The ancient Champa Kingdom was a Hinduised, matriarchal culture, which at its height occupied all of central Vietnam and large sections of present-day Laos and Cambodia. Had a few wars turned out differently, Champa might have become Indochina's fourth country. Champa was eventually reduced to its southernmost province of Panduranga (modern Binh Thuan and Ninh Thuan provinces). While there was later a mass exodus of Cham to Cambodia, and the kingdom was eventually dissolved by the Vietnamese King Minh Mang in 1832, the remaining Cham retain a thriving culture today.

Champa's architectural treasures are evident in their ancient red-brick temples scattered along the coast of Vietnam. In Panduranga alone there were dozens of such temples. Most here are mere vestiges, unmarked and lacking protection from any organised conservation effort.

PHAN THIET

The city of **Phan Thiet** is the capital of Binh Thuan Province. Its original Cham name was 'Hamu Lithit'. Today, it is best known for the beach at Mui Ne and as the home of Vietnam's best *nuoc mam* (fish sauce), and the centre of dragon fruit production.

Thap Po Shanu

Begin your tour at 8am at **Thap Po Shanu** ❶ (Km5 Nguyen Thong; 8am–

Above from far left: Poshanu Cham tower near Mui Ne; strolling along Mui Ne Beach.

5pm; charge) on a hilltop overlooking Phan Thiet, just west of Mui Ne. Here three temple towers now stand, and vestiges of several other structures, all built in the eighth century. This temple site is the southernmost in Vietnam, and one of the oldest standing Cham temples yet identified. According to scholars, it was originally devoted to Shiva, as indicated by the pair of phallic stone *linga-yoni* in the main tower.

Po Shanu overlooks the **Phu Hai River**, which changes names to Cai and Song Quao as it flows upstream to the highlands. Cham lords established their quasi-independent territories along important river systems like this one, all along the coast of Vietnam. The Cham built temples along the rivers as their civilisations developed further upstream. The author has recently discovered three temple ruins, and government archaeologists have located two others along this river system alone. There are probably many more.

As you walk down the hill, be sure to stop in the **gift shop** for authentic pottery and textiles made by Cham craftswomen. There is also a fine gem and rock shop selling local stones.

Mui Ne

Drive east along **Mui Ne Beach** ❷, the resort and water-sports capital of Vietnam. This area (the real name of the area is Ham Tien; technically Mui Ne is just the name of the village on the cape at the end) first saw tourism when meteorologists designated it the best site in Vietnam to see the solar eclipse in 1995. Now tourists – many of them Russian – are coming to swim,

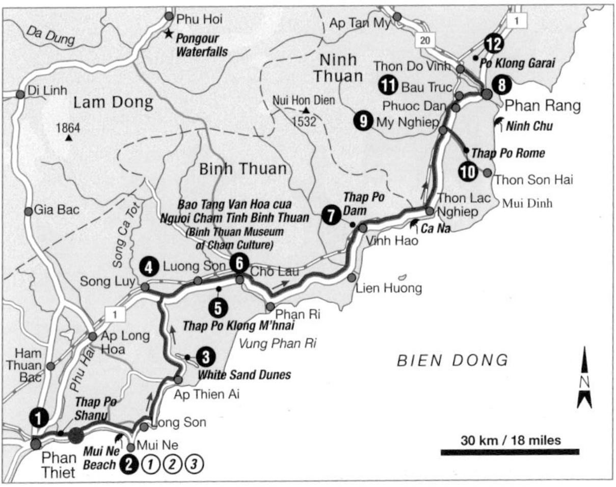

Above: kite-surfing at Mui Ne Beach.

sunbathe, enjoy the many bars and restaurants and go kite-boarding.

You'll pass a myriad of dining choices along the strip, the best of which include **Forest Restaurant**, **Vietnam Home** and **Joe's Café** (all on the left side), see ①–③. Get breakfast along the beach and consider getting take-away sandwiches from Joe's, as you'll be limited to sparse options of Vietnamese street food the rest of the way.

White Sand Dunes

Drive north from Mui Ne Beach for 33km (20 miles) along the coast. On the way to the dunes, it's hard to miss the **titanium mining** operations along the highway. Some of the world's richest deposits are located in these dunes. Eventually you'll come to a beautiful lake system backed by immense dunes. Take the right fork along the lake and stop at the park entrance.

The **White Sand Dunes** ❸ are an immense Saharan range of undulating golden and snow-white dunes. Nestled at their base are two large reservoirs and a series of smaller lakes, which offer excellent opportunities to watch local birdlife. A number of small horses wonder the shores, enhancing the ambience. There are also village kids standing by, waiting to rent sleds to visitors for 'dune surfing'.

After a bit of fun, drive back west along the lake shore. Between the two lakes sits a **new shrine** under the trees. Here once stood an ancient Cham temple. Now the local Vietnamese residents worship the Cham goddess Po Nagar by another name: Tien Y A-Na. Continue driving north 14.5km (9 miles) to meet Highway 1.

SONG LUY CITADEL

Turn left (west) on Highway 1 and drive for 5km (3 miles), watching closely for signs designating that you are in Song Luy. Take the first right on the dirt road going north to enter Song Luy proper. As you approach you will see orange citadel walls weaving between the houses.

According to extensive research by the author, **Song Luy** ❹ (meaning 'River Fortification') is the site of **Ban Canan** (Bal Canar), the ancient imperial capital of Panduranga and last capital city of the Champa Empire. Ban Canan may have existed as Panduranga's capital for the better part of a millennium, but Po (King) Chai Paran moved Champa's imperial capital from Virapura (modern Phan Rang) to Ban Canan in 1653, at a time when the kingdom was waning thanks to Vietnamese southward expansion. The area was a key battleground during the Tay Son Rebellion of the late 1700s, which may account for why the citadel 'shows greater knowledge in the art of fortification than any other' in Vietnam. Although the victor of the rebellion, King Gia Long, awarded control of the area to the loyal Cham royal family, in 1822 his descendant,

Sun and heat care
During the day, always wear sunscreen, a hat and bring plenty of water. This region is the driest in all of Southeast Asia.

the emperor Minh Mang, dissolved all vestiges of Cham autonomy and Ban Canan fell into obscurity.

The citadel with built on the south banks of the **Luy River**, with earthen walls 7 to 10m (23 to 32ft) tall. Today they stand 1 to 6m (3 to 20ft). The total circumference is about 4km (2½ miles). Walk around the city and climb the ramparts for views of the town and countryside. Residents of this city are, interestingly, not Cham but ethnic Nung and Hoa, strategically relocated from the far north by the government. The homes of the Nung are wooden, unlike those of their Vietnamese neighbours, with tiny balconies. Flags hang in their doorways with Chinese characters emblazoned. Be sure to stroll through the market at the centre of the village and try some of the unique northern cuisine, like *bun rieu cua* (rice noodle soup with crab meatballs).

THAP PO KLONG M'HNAI

From Song Luy, backtrack and drive east on Highway 1 for 4km (6 miles). You'll pass through the town of Luong Son. As the road veers left, on a hilltop to your right overlooking the river you will see the 17th-century **Thap Po Klong M'hnai** ❺, a temple complex dedicated to one of the last kings of Champa, along with his Cham wife and Vietnamese concubine. Three shrines stand here now, though originally there were five structures. Climb up the hill and have a look, but be aware that the complex is usually locked, so you'll have to view from outside the gate. If you happen to find yourself on the other side of the short fence, take a peek at the statues of the royal family, each inside their temple shrines.

BINH THUAN MUSEUM OF CHAM CULTURE

Heading another 14km (8 miles) east on Highway 1, you'll come to a crossroads in the middle of the town of **Cho**

Above from far left: a reclining Buddha near Phan Thiet; dragon fruit; Phan Thiet water tower; White Sand Dunes.

Food and Drink

① FOREST RESTAURANT (RUNG)
67 Nguyen Dinh Chieu Street; tel: 062-384 7589; www.forestrestaurant.com; daily L & D; $$$
The Forest Restaurant resembles a ruined Cham temple reclaimed by the jungle. Most of the staff are ethnic Cham, and live Cham music and dance shows go on all night. The menu includes traditional Vietnamese favourites and seafood.

② VIETNAM HOME
125A Nguyen Dinh Chieu Street; tel: 062-384 7687; daily B, L & D; $$$
Vietnam Home is a traditional Vietnamese restaurant within a festive, bamboo treehouse setting. The menu features seafood prominently, as well as local dishes like grilled lizard and cobra. Live hill-tribe music shows are featured occasionally.

③ JOE'S CAFÉ
139 Nguyen Dinh Chieu Street; tel: 062-374 3447; daily B, L & D; $$
Joe's is the only local venue open 24 hours, offering Italian coffee, exceptional pizzas, burgers, pasta and a wide selection of sandwiches and breakfast dishes. The quality of food and service is very high. Live pop-rock music is performed nightly after 8pm.

Above: King Po Rome depicted in the likeness of Shiva on the altar in the main temple of Po Rome; a rare symbol in Cham culture is the *mukhalinga* – a *linga* with a human face.

Lau. On the northeast corner is the new **Binh Thuan Museum of Cham Culture** ❻ (Bao Tang Van Hoa cua Nguoi Cham Tinh Binh Thuan). If you have time, it is worth a stop. Be aware, however, that there are no regular hours, and the government-appointed administrator will haggle over the 'donation' required for entry. It's best to arrive from Tuesday to Sunday, 8–11am or 2–4pm. Agree on an admission price of about 20,000VND per person before entry. The first floor of the museum contains replicas of statuary and items of worship from Binh Thuan Province and other Cham sites to the north. The second floor contains exhibits of costumes, musical instruments, baskets and pottery, as well as replicas of the royal wardrobe and crowns.

THAP PO DAM

It's another 8km (5 miles) to the town of **Phan Ri**. Phan Ri was one of the most important ports in Panduranga, known as 'Pa-Rik'. Many Cham kings, queens and court officials are buried in a veritable 'valley of the kings' here, though the royal cemeteries are unmarked and have recently fallen victim to looting.

Another 19km (12 miles) brings you through the town of **Lien Huong,** where the road veers north towards the mountains and meets the sea. Drive 4km (2½ miles) north, and just before passing between the low mountains, take an unmarked dirt road to the left, veering north. You will cross a bridge over a canal and then the train tracks. Clearly situated on the mountain slopes you will see a set of Cham temples.

Thap Po Dam ❼ (daylight hours; free) was built in the ninth century and as such is one of the oldest standing temple complexes in Vietnam. It was originally a group of six temples, but now only three are standing. Legend says that this temple was built as part of a temple construction contest between two kings. Strangely, it is the only Cham temple complex to face southwards rather than towards the east.

Be careful not to disturb the rare Bray's Champa geckos (*Gekko champai*, sp.nov) that nest in the ruins and lay their eggs on the temple walls. These giant geckos were recently discovered and are endemic to this valley.

PHAN RANG

Back on the highway, it's another 50km (31 miles) north to the city of **Phan Rang** ❽. The twin cities of Phan Rang and Thap Cham comprise the provincial capital of Ninh Thuan Province, and are the focal point of the modern Cham homeland. The local economy is based on fishing, rice farming and, increasingly, tourism.

Check into your hotel in Phan Rang and get something to eat. Phan Rang lacks a good selection of restaurants

Da Lat wæine

Ninh Thuan Province is covered in vineyards. The grapes for Da Lat's famous wine are actually grown here. The Cham also raise a lot of goats as well as flocks of sheep. The latter are seen almost nowhere else in Vietnam.

catering to foreign visitors. The best option is to sample street food either at the **roundabout** at the intersection of Le Loi and Ngo Gia Tu streets, or the food stalls around the **central market** on Thong Nhat Street. Both locations are prominent landmarks. The roundabout is strictly outdoor seating, while the market has indoor and outdoor stalls. Local specialities include *banh xeo* (seafood pancakes), *sup cua* (crab soup) and *banh cuon* (fresh spring rolls).

Thap Po Rome and My Nghiep

Rise early in the morning, taking breakfast at the Central Market, and drive south on Highway 1, to the town of Phuoc Dan. At the intersection with road 703, take a brief detour, turning left to visit the craft village of **My Nghiep** ❾. Here you can observe traditional Cham weaving and purchase beautiful blankets and clothing. Afterwards backtrack and cross the highway, heading north through Nhuan Duc village. About 15km (10 miles) south of Phan Rang on a hilltop sits the temple-tower of **Thap Po Rome** ❿ (daylight hours; 'free' with tip for caretaker), named after a king of Champa who ruled from 1629 to 1651 and died a captive of the Vietnamese. The tower is one of the last built by the Cham, in the early 17th century. Four images of Po Rome sit in ascending enclaves on each side of the temple. Inside Po Rome is presented in the likeness of Shiva. A statue of his wife sits beside him.

Thap Po Klong Garai and Bau Truc

From Po Rome backtrack, heading north on road 703. Stop on the way at **Bau Truc** ⓫ craft village to see how Cham make traditional pottery without benefit of a kick wheel (and purchase a few pieces while you are there). Continue down the road and then turn west, driving another 7km (4 miles) towards Da Lat on Highway 27. You'll clearly see the three 14th-century towers, known as **Po Klong Garai** ⓬ (Thap Cham; daily 8am–6pm; charge) standing on an arid hill. The temple was built to worship King Po Klong Garai, who was acclaimed for constructing a much-needed local irrigation system. The entrance to the largest tower is graced with a dancing, six-armed Po Klong Garai represented as Shiva, and inside sits a statue of the bull Nandin.

After you've explored the temple, head back to Phan Rang for a late lunch.

Above from far left: Po Rome temple-tower; workshop in Bau Truc.

Below: pottery shaped by hand, without the use of machines, in Bau Truc.

5

NHA TRANG

Beaches. Nightlife. Scuba diving. These four words encapsulate the Nha Trang experience for most travellers. Discover the hidden charm of Vietnam's favourite party town and visit the many museums and aquariums, sampling rich ethnic culture along the way.

DISTANCE 7km (4 miles) by car
TIME A full day
START Po Nagar Cham Towers
END Vinpearl Land Amusement Park
POINTS TO NOTE
Nha Trang is best reached from Mui Ne, Phan Rang or Da Lat by bus. From Danang, the train or a flight to nearby Cam Ranh is advised. Nha Trang is a family-friendly city with some of the best bars, restaurants and hotels outside HCMC and Hanoi. A hire car, motorbike or taxi will be necessary for this tour.

Know before you buy
Unfortunately Nha Trang has a proliferation of souvenirs made from threatened and endangered species. Anything made from shark's fin, dried seahorses or bleached coral, snake wine, sea turtle shells, bear claws or leopard teeth should be avoided.

Nha Trang is the ideal place to break a journey, relax and soak up the sun. The city has grown from a relatively run-down little beach town to an internationally recognised vacation destination in just the last decade. Nha Trang received worldwide attention in 2008 when it hosted the Miss Universe Pageant and has continued as a focal point for Vietnam's high-profile events since.

Nha Trang is blessed with a beautiful **municipal beach** which fronts almost the entire city, along Tran Phu Street. There are always visitors basking in the warm sun and cool breezes at popular beach bars, and plenty of activities, whether jet skiing, sailing, windsurfing, parasailing or spending the day at an island amusement park.

PO NAGAR CHAM TEMPLE

Begin your tour where it all started: the ancient ruins of **Po Nagar** ❶ (2/4 Street, Vinh Hai Ward; tel: 058-383 1569; daily 6am–6pm; charge), on a hill above the **Cai River**. Only four of the sanctuary's original eight temples, all of which face east, remain standing. These were constructed over a long span of time between the seventh and 12th centuries. The 22 pillars and steep steps leading up to the main tower hint at the grandeur of the original temple.

The main tower is dedicated to the Cham goddess Po Yang Inu Nagar (worshipped by local Vietnamese as the goddess Thien Y A-Na), the 'Holy Mother' of the kingdom and

considered by Cham to be a female manifestation of the Hindu god Shiva. Her statue resides in the main temple, but it was decapitated during French rule, and the original head is now in the Guimet Museum in Paris.

Ethnic Cham performers from Phan Rang present live traditional music and dance from 7.30am–11am and 2.30–4.30pm daily. Shops behind the temples sell authentic Cham crafts. Some of the textiles are woven in a traditional loom, on-site.

DAM MARKET

Some of Nha Trang's most interesting French colonial architecture and crumbling old Chinese taverns – as much as 200 years old – can be seen around **Dam Market** ❷ near the Cai River. To get there, head south on Ha Ra Bridge via Street 2 Thang 4 and turn left. This former Chinese quarter is the most underrated part of town. The bustling market is surprisingly un-touristed, and a welcome contrast to the rest of the modernised city, with its rustic and spontaneous atmosphere. It's a great place to snack while you explore: food is everywhere.

The Pasteur Institute

From Dam Market, head east to Tran Phu Street, where you will find the **Pasteur Institute** ❸ (Vien Pasteur). The institute was founded in 1895 by Dr Alexandre Yersin, a French microbiologist, military doctor, explorer and overall Renaissance man who previously worked at the Pasteur

Above from far left: Po Nagar tower; Rainbow Divers.

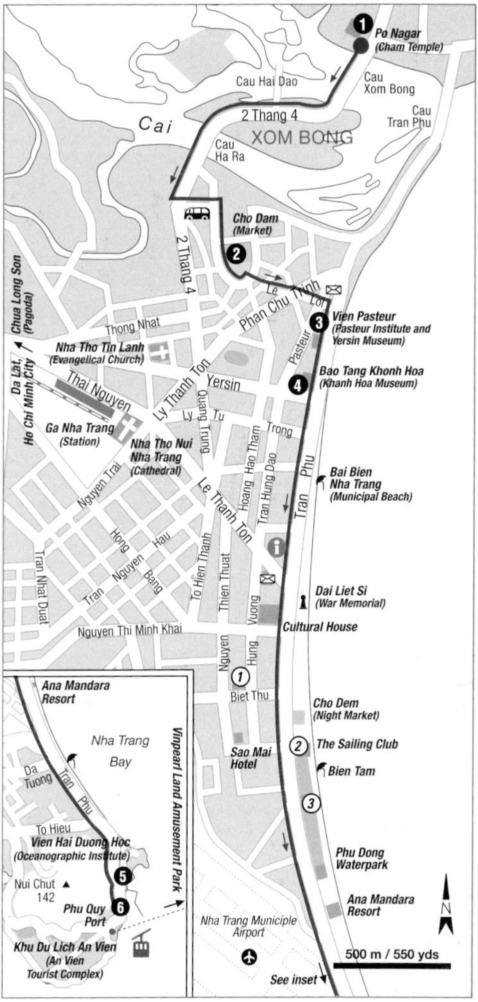

Scam crackdown
Signs posted at Dam Market entrance are remarkably candid: 'Notice for Foreign Visitors... Please deal with the stall owners directly. Do not trust the interpretation and recommendation of the strange guides.' Outgoing strangers in markets are often running scams.

Institute in Paris, where he helped Emile Roux discover the diphtheria bacterium *(see box, below)*. Today the Institute still produces vaccines and carries out research, though with a very limited budget.

The small **Alexandre Yersin Museum** (10D Tran Phu; tel: 058-822 355; Mon–Fri 7.30–11am, 2–4.30pm; charge), displays many of Yersin's personal effects, furniture, documents and antique laboratory gadgets (including an enormous telescope). Many of his old books are kept in the library on display. This is the only portion of the institute open to the public.

Dr Alexandre Yersin

Alexandre Yersin arrived in Nha Trang in 1891 and was one of the first Europeans extensively to explore the Central Highlands and Mekong region south of Saigon. Yersin was also responsible for introducing Brazilian rubber trees and *quinquina* plantations – quinine-producing trees – to Vietnam at Suoi Dau, about 25km (15 miles) southwest of Nha Trang. He is buried here among his rubber trees, with a pagoda built nearby to worship him.

In 1894 Yersin was sent to Hong Kong by the French government and the Pasteur Institute to investigate an outbreak of bubonic plague. He soon discovered the link between rats, fleas, and eventually the bacterial cause (later renamed *Yersinia pestis* in his honour). In 1895 he returned to Nha Trang and built a laboratory to manufacture the serum for the disease. In 1905 the lab became an official branch of the Pasteur Institute.

KHANH HOA PROVINCIAL MUSEUM

Almost next door to the Pasteur Institute, the small **Khanh Hoa Museum** ❹ (Bao Tang Khonh Hoa; 16D Tran Phu Street; tel: 058-822 277; Tue–Fri 8am–11am, 2–5pm; free) can be explored thoroughly in about 15 minutes. The left wing contains relics from the Xom Con (*c.*3,000 years old), Dong Son (*c.*2000BC–AD200) and Champa (peak between seventh and 12th centuries) cultures. The most unusal item is the 3,000-year-old stone lithograph (a musical instrument similar to a marimba). Notably absent are any of the otherwise ubiquitous exhibits about the previous wars or Uncle Ho found in most Vietnamese museums.

Afterwards, have lunch like a scuba diver, and consider (or at least dream about) signing up for some lessons at **Rainbow Divers**, see 🍴①. Get there by going south on Tran Phu, then turn right on Biet Thu, stopping at the corner of Hung Vong.

OCEANOGRAPHIC INSTITUTE

After lunch head south about 5km (3 miles) on Tran Phu Street, passing the

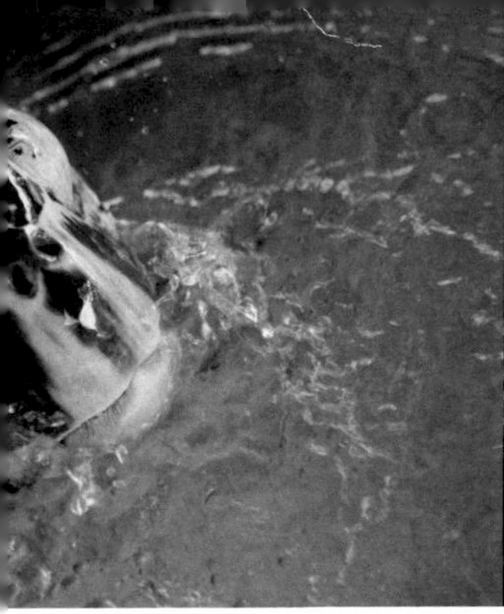

Sailing Club, Louisiane and Bao Dai Villas (former holiday home of the last emperor). Sandwiched between the Bao Dai villas and Phu Quy Port, the **Oceanographic Institute** ❺ (1 Cau Da; tel: 058-590 036; daily 6am–6pm; charge) in Cau Da District was founded in 1923 and housed in a large French colonial complex. The institute has about a dozen large, open aquarium tanks. Most notable are the prowling sharks, inquisitive rays and seemingly oblivious sea turtles. A dozen smaller tanks are housed inside, showcasing bizarre reef fish and seahorses. The main building houses a massive collection of preserved specimens. Impressive still are the giant humpback whale and dugong skeletons, as well as the entire pickled dugong, which might turn a few stomachs.

VINPEARL LAND AND AQUARIUM

Seen from Nha Trang's municipal beach, Hon Tre (Bamboo Island) is home to the **Vinpearl Land Amusement Park** (Hon Tre; tel: 058-958 188; www.vinpearlland.com; daily 8am–10pm; charge) and Vinpearl Resort. A gondola extending 3,320m (10,892ft) to the island departs from the **Phu Quy Port** ❻, about 500m (1640ft) south of the Oceanographic Institute, and delivers visitors to the centre of the amusement park. The park contains a number of carnival rides and a roller coaster, games area, water park, outdoor shopping center and several restaurants.

The crowning feature of the park is the modern **Underwater World** with more than 20 freshwater and marine tanks of varying sizes, including a very impressive walk-through tank featuring sharks, rays, morays and a large variety of reef animals.

After you've had your fun, head back to the **Sailing Club** or **Louisiane**, see 🍴② and 🍴③, for dinner and some nightlife.

Above from far left: Alexandre Yersin Museum; turtle at the Oceanographic Institute; the Aquarium.

Food and Drink

① RAINBOW DIVERS
90A Hung Vuong; tel: 058-352 4351; www.divevietnam.com; daily B, L & D; $$$
The head office of Vietnam's top dive shop has an excellent bar and restaurant. The cosy all-wood interior feels like the cabin of a ship. The menu includes steak sandwiches, burgers, pizza, pasta, Australian meat pies and steaks, and English fish and chips.

② THE SAILING CLUB
72–74 Tran Phu; tel: 058-382 6528; www.sailingclubvietnam.com; daily B, L & D; $$$$
The Sailing Club is one of the best-known expat haunts in Vietnam. Directly on the beach and open late, Sailing Club is an amalgamation of several unique eateries and bars, including the signature Sandals Restaurant. Menus include Indian, Italian, Western and Asian fusion.

③ LOUISIANE BREWHOUSE
Lot 29, Tran Phu; tel: 058-352 1948; www.louisianebrewhouse.com.vn; daily B, L & D; $$$$
The Louisiane is the most chilled-out yet opulent beach hangout in town. The beachside restaurant with swimming pool offers mostly Vietnamese seafood, with some steaks, burgers, pizza and sushi thrown in. The microbrewery beers are a must-try.

6

DA LAT

An old colonial mountain resort, Da Lat was a favourite getaway for not only the French, but also the last emperor, Bao Dai. Escape the coastal heat, enjoy the abundance of fresh, local produce and stroll along Lake Xuan Huong below some of Vietnam's best colonial architecture.

DISTANCE 10km (6 miles)
TIME A full day
START Da Lat Central Market
END Dalat Palace Golf Club
POINTS TO NOTE
Da Lat is the most walkable city in Vietnam. This tour is suitable for the entire family, and though the walk is up and down gentle hills, it is not challenging. This tour requires a mix of walking and rides in taxis or motorbikes. Da Lat also serves as the starting point for the Central Highlands road trip.

Da Lat is the capital of Lam Dong Province, resting at an elevation of 1500m (4921ft), on the Langbiang Plateau. The city is ideally situated as a vacation hub with major highways leading conveniently to HCMC, Phan Thiet, Phan Rang, Nha Trang and Buon Ma Thuat. With an average annual temperature of 17°C (63°F), Da Lat is Vietnam's most popular fair-weather retreat and the nation's top honeymoon destination.

The original inhabitants of the area were the K'ho tribe, divided into the Lat and Chil clans. Da Lat literally means 'River of the Lat People,' although much of the clan relocated to nearby Lat village as Da Lat grew. In addition to the K'ho, the Ma and Churu tribes also inhabit the hills surrounding Da Lat. Although largely forced to assimilate by the government, occasionally people can be seen walking about in quasi-traditional dress with large baskets hanging on their backs.

Dr Alexandre Yersin *(see p.48)* was the first European to survey the area in 1893, under the authority of Paul Doumer, the French governor-general of Indochina. Considered the founder of Da Lat, he recommended a hill station and sanatorium be built here to take advantage of the mild climate and beautiful scenery.

Local Specialities
Da Lat wine – available simply in red or white – is one of Vietnam's staple products, as are the plethora of dried and candied fruits. Strawberries are another signature Da Lat product, which are candied, turned to jam, concentrated, fermented into wine or blended into tasty fruit shakes. *See also p.44.*

DA LAT CENTRAL MARKET

Begin your tour at the **Da Lat Central Market** ❶. It is set in the deep hollow of a tall hillside and surrounded by rows of cafés and shops selling flowers, wine and candied fruit.

Food is the highlight here. The second floor of the middle building is devoted entirely to food stalls: mostly rice meals with local specialities, and *che*, a desert made with sweetened beans and candied fruit. The stairs and ramps leading to the market are also flanked with vendors in the evening, selling grilled meats, corn, sweet potatoes, and rice crackers topped with quail-egg omelettes; *sua dau nanh* (hot, fresh soy milk); *banh cam* (sesame doughnuts filled with green-bean paste); sweet waffles stuffed with cheese and pork; and bowls of steamed snails. The take-away specialities sold throughout the market include dried and candied fruits, wines and deer jerky. Grab some breakfast here.

The market is bustling well before 6am and remains open long past 11pm. On Saturdays and Sundays from 7–10pm, the streets surrounding the market are closed to vehicles and a carnival atmosphere ensues with an influx of pedestrians, souvenir pedlars, food vendors and street-side clothing auctioneers.

DA LAT CATHEDRAL

From the market, walk south on Le Dai Hanh (the lake will be on your left), then straight ahead is the tan- and cream-colored **Da Lat Cathedral** ❷ (Nha Tho Con Ga or 'Rooster Church'; Mon–Sat Mass 5.15am and 5.15pm, Sun Mass 5.15am, 7am, 8.30am, 4pm and 6pm). The cathedral was built in 1942, with stained-glass windows made by Louis Balmet, in

Above from far left: fresh produce and other goodies at Da Lat Central Market.

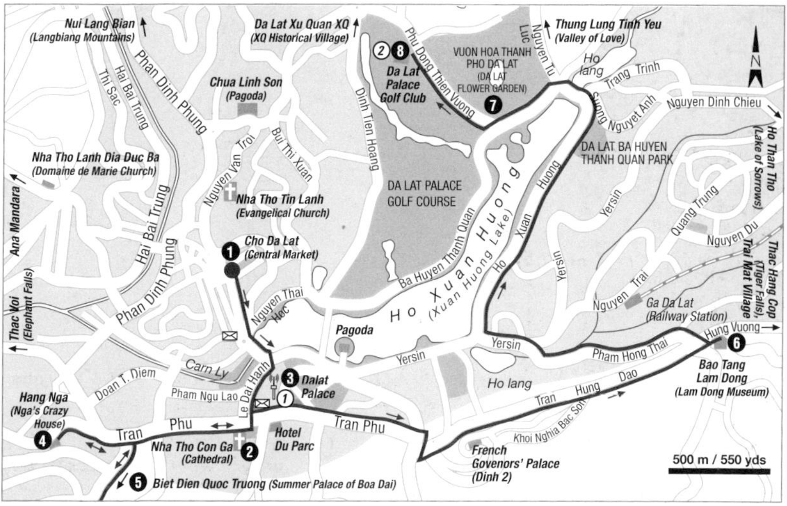

Above:
Nga's Crazy House.

Grenoble, France. The rooster weather vane on top of the steeple lends the church its nickname.

DA LAT PALACE AND HOTEL DU PARC

Da Lat was originally built around the grand Langbian Palace Hotel, now known as the **Da Lat Palace** ❸. Construction of the hotel began in 1902 and finished 20 years later (at the time, travel from the coast took more than a week, making construction difficult). The **Hotel Du Parc** followed in 1932. Both retain much of their original architectural charm. Both hotels sit to the left of the cathedral, on either side of Tran Phu Street. **Le Café de la Poste**, see ①, between the two hotels (and owned by the same company), makes a great breakfast or lunch stop.

NGA'S CRAZY HOUSE

Head west on Tran Phu Street now, then turn south (left) at the triangular roundabout onto 3 Thang 2 Street. Finally take a right on Huynh Thuc Khang. For anyone travelling with children, or those who played in treehouses themselves as a child, **Nga's Crazy House** ❹ (Hang Nga; 3 Huynh Thuc Khang; tel: 063-382 2070; daily 7am–6pm; charge) is a whimsical and inspiring architectural delight for the whole family. The never-ending house is continuously being added to, with tunnels, stairways and halls meandering into secret rooms, towers and reading nooks, occupied by giant kangaroos, giraffes, eagles and bears.

BAO DAI'S SUMMER PALACE

Walking less than a kilometre further south on 3 Thang 2 Street, and turning left on Trieu Viet Vuong Street, brings you to the **Summer Palace of Bao Dai** ❺ (Biet Dien Quoc Truong; Duong Trieu Viet Vuong; tel: 063-382 6858; daily 7.30am–11am, 1.30–4pm; charge), Vietnam's last emperor, which was built between 1933 and 1938. This is the third of the palaces (designated Dinh I, Dinh II and Dinh III) belonging to Bao Dai in Da Lat, although the other two are not currently open to the public. It's said that all three are connected by tunnels so that the emperor could secretly visit his mistresses in each one.

LAM DONG MUSEUM

Grab a taxi or motorbike and head back to Tran Phu Street, which turns into Tran Hung Dao and then Hun Vuong. Da Lat's **Lam Dong Museum** ❻ (Bao Tang Lam Dong; 04 Hung Vuong; tel: 063-382 2339; daily 7.30am–11.30am, 1.30–4.30pm; charge) is an excellent museum, recognised by the United Nations for

Above from far left: bust of Emperor Bao Dai in the third palace; Lam Dong Museum; Da Lat Palace golf course.

its extensive collection of musical gongs, used by the local K'ho, Ma and Churu minorities. Exhibits also include a very impressive taxidermy collection of local wildlife; relics from the Funan Empire, excavated at Cat Tien National Park; artefacts found in recent excavations from yet-unidentified cultures; and full-sized Ma and K'ho longhouses, decorated with musical instruments, weapons and common household items.

XUAN HUONG LAKESIDE

Catch a taxi or motorbike to any stretch along **Xuan Huong Lake** to continue your walk. Formerly part of the town's colonial-era golf course before it was flooded, the lake sprawls through the heart of the town. The surrounding hills, villas and pine forests provide a lovely backdrop. The lake was drained for dredging in early 2010, and is scheduled to be refilled by mid-2012.

Da Lat Flower Garden

Walk to the north side of the lake and visit the **Da Lat Flower Garden** ❼ (2 Tran Nhan Tong; tel: 063-355 3545; 7am–6pm; charge). The best time to visit the gardens is during the annual **Da Lat Flower Festival**, usually held for a week in November, December or January (dates and activities vary from year to year), when there are beautiful flower displays in the gardens, surrounding a small lake.

Da Lat Palace Golf Club

On the northern banks, a golf course originally built for the last emperor, Bao Dai, has been renovated and expanded into the lovely **Da Lat Palace Golf Club** ❽. The 18-hole championship course is a sister location to the Ocean Dunes Golf Club in Phan Thiet, and voted the number 1 course in Vietnam by *Golf Digest* (2007). They also have a great restaurant to watch the sunset over the green, see ②.

Food and Drink

① LE CAFÉ DE LA POSTE
Tran Phu Street; tel: 063-382 5444; daily B, L & D; $$$$
This charming French-style café serves a select menu of sandwiches, pasta, Asian and French dishes. Service is friendly, and meals are prepared with great care. Even the toasted ham and cheese sandwich is a memorable treat. The buffet breakfast is excellent.

② DA LAT PALACE GOLF CLUB
Phu Dong Thien Vuong Street; tel: 063-382 1201; daily B, L & D; $$$$
Set in the original colonial clubhouse, the restaurant serves Tex-Mex, Korean, Japanese, Thai and Vietnamese specialities. The home-made chips and salsa, buffalo wings and chicken fingers are all top-notch. Outdoor seating offers a lovely view of the greens and lake.

Discouraging poaching
Avoid the tiger and bear claws in the market shops, as purchasing them encourages poaching of endangered wildlife around Langbiang Mountain. The teeth in the shops tend to be plastic fakes, but the claws are generally real.

7 CENTRAL HIGHLANDS

Spend a few days on the open road, exploring Vietnam's mountainous interior by car or motorbike. The region is populated by hill-tribe minorities in a landscape of tea and coffee plantations, peppered with waterfalls and elephant herds.

DISTANCE 373km (232 miles)
TIME 3 days
START Da Lat
END Buon Ma Thuot
POINTS TO NOTE
This tour forms a continuation of tour 6 and a possible bridge to tour 5. This road trip can be taken by private car or motorbike, ideally with a guide. Da Lat's 'Easyriders', a loose association of motorbike guides, are a popular option. Just stand on the street above Da Lat's Central Market and one will find you. Usually no particular preparations are needed when you travel with a guide; they tend to take care of all your needs. The most popular tour company is Phat Tire Ventures, 73 Truong Cong Dinh; www.phattireventures.com; tel: 063-382 9422.

Political hotspot
Minority groups of the Central Highlands – many Catholic and Protestant – have always had a particularly independent streak. Periodic protests, centring on Buon Ma Thuot, have made this a politically volatile area, and some places (including most of Gia Lai Province, and portions of western Dak Lak and Kon Tum) are off-limits to foreigners.

Vietnam's Central Highlands include the provinces of Gia Nghia, Lam Dong, Dak Lak, Gia Lai and Kon Tum. The area has historically been home to many ethnic minorities, including the Ma, K'ho, Jarai, Ede and Bahnar. Many of them, particularly in the north, were subjects of the former Champa Kingdom, but gradually brought under the dominion of the French and eventually the Vietnamese.

The highlands are a major agricultural centre for Vietnam, where crops include coffee, tea, black pepper, vegetables, flowers and corn. Unlike coastal areas, relatively little rice is grown here. The cities of the Central Highlands are quite new. Most were built by the French and continued as American military bases during the war.

ON FROM DA LAT

Leave early in the morning (the earlier the better) from **Da Lat ❶**. The first day of driving 156km (97 miles) north on Highway 27 is mostly about enjoying the scenery through tea and coffee plantations, with quick stops for photos.

Elephant Falls

Elephant Falls ❷ (Thac Voi; free), 30km (19 miles) west of Da Lat, is a favourite stop for most countryside tours from Dalat. The dramatic rock

Above from far left: Elephant Falls; a cable-car ride near Da Lat offers panoramas of villages and mountain forests.

formations are just as interesting as the falls themselves; which look like a movie set from Peter Jackson's *King Kong*. It's a bit of a climb down to the bottom of the falls, but natural-looking stairs have been skilfully built into the rocks to make the way easier. A shop above the falls sells beautiful hand-woven K'ho blankets and crafts, all made on-site.

Farms

On your way to Lak Lake, you will pass many different **farms** specialising in roses and other flowers, mushrooms, silk, black pepper, coffee and tea plantations, and even rice-wine distilleries. To visit these, it is essential to have a guide, as they are not signposted and do not have their own guides to provide tours.

LAK LAKE

You will probably arrive at **Lak Lake** ❸ in time for dinner at **Lak Resort Floating Restaurant**, see ①. The shores of Lak Lake are inhabited by displaced members of the M'nong tribe, relocated here from the north by the government. The M'nong number about 50,000 and are matriarchal. The M'nong have been famed elephant-catchers for hundreds of years, although their elephants are

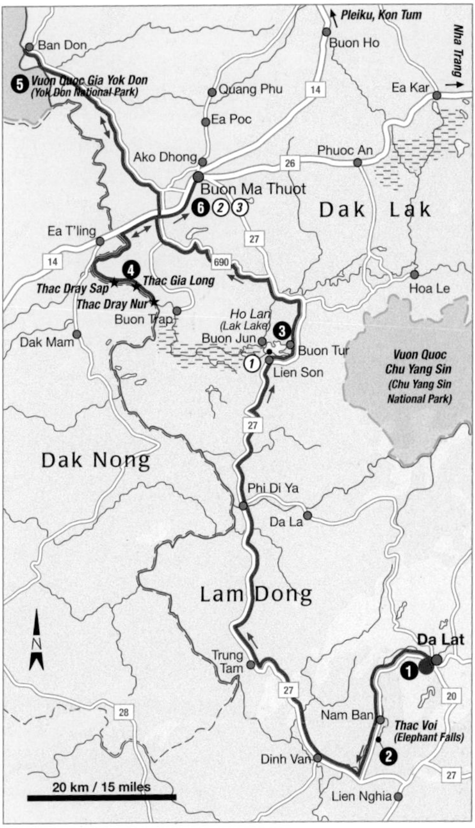

Food and Drink

① LAK RESORT FLOATING RESTAURANT

Lien Son village, near Buon Jun, Lak Lake; tel: 0500-358 6184; daily B, L & D; $$

In a scenic location on Lak Lake, the restaurant is an ideal spot for lunch or to watch the sunset over a beer or two. The menu is mainly Vietnamese with a few back-packer favourites. The set menu is good value.

Above: radish and strawberry farms in the lush highland countryside.

now used for tourist rides rather than dragging logs from the forest.

Night in a Longhouse

Spend the night in one of the immense wooden M'nong longhouses on the lake (they are available for evening rentals at the tourism office in front of Buong Jun village). Be advised that sleeping is on a mat on the floor, under a mosquito net, and bathrooms are a communal outhouse. Otherwise, opt for luxury and spend the evening in Emperor Bao Dai's hunting lodge, now a hotel *(see p.110)*.

Boat Rides

Rise early the next morning and explore the lake by dugout. The canoes are painstakingly hollowed out from tree trunks by axe. Two people can sit in the boats, with a driver in the back. This is a good way to view the mountain scenery and watch the village kids riding their water buffalos as they swim across the lake.

Villages

A number of villages can be visited by boat. The best Ede village to visit is **Buon Tur**, while **Buon Jun** is inhabited by M'nong. Villagers live in tall longhouses. Families depart in a mass exodus early each morning to herd cattle, fish in the lake, or gather resources from the countryside, returning home at dinner time.

DRAY SAP, DRAY NUR AND GIA LONG WATERFALLS

After a quick lunch, drive north on Highway 27. At the 22km (13½-mile) marker, south of Buon Ma Thuot, take Road 690 west to Highway 14. Drive 8km (5 miles) south, then take the marked left turnoff 3km (2 miles) to the entrance of **Dray Sap, Dray Nur and Gia Long waterfalls** ❹ (tel: 0500-385 0123; daily 7am–5pm; charge). There are toilets and a café at the entrance.

Originating from Cu Yang Sin Mountain, the three waterfalls of Dray Sap, Dray Nur and Gia Long form a 100m (328 ft) wide cascade. They are particularly stunning in the wet season, although Dray Sap and Dray Nur are impressive even in the dry season.

YUK DON NATIONAL PARK

Drive another hour north and spend the evening inside **Yok Don National Park** ❺ (Vuon Quoc Gia Yok Don, Buon Don District; tel: 500-378 3049; email: yokdonecotourism@vnn.vn; charge). Limited dining is available at the park ranger station, or the food stalls in **Ban Don village**, just a couple of kilometres further up the road.

This 115,545-hectare (45,760-acre) wildlife reserve contains at least 63 species of mammals and 250 species of birds. More than 15

of these animals are listed as endangered. There are known to be around 50 Asian elephants (including rare white elephants), 10 tigers, giant muntjac, Samba deer, golden jackal, leopard and green peafowl living in the park.

Rise early the next morning for an elephant and boat ride. Elephant riding costs $40 for two hours and river-boat rides are $20 for one hour (trekking in the park is also available with a guide, at $15 for three hours). Plan to leave the park by noon.

BUON MA THUOT

Drive two hours southeast and arrive at **Buon Ma Thuot** ❻, the capital of Dak Lak Province, as well as the capital of Vietnam's coffee production. Have a late lunch at **Thang Loi Restaurant** on 1 Phan Chu Trinh Street, see ②.

Museum of Ethnology

After lunch, head just south of the city centre to the corner of Le Duan and Y Nong Streets. Dak Lak's **Museum of Ethnology** (Y Nong Street; Tue–Sun 7.30–11am, 2–5pm; charge) has one of the finest collections of Central Highlands hill-tribe crafts and relics, outside the Hanoi Museum of Ethnology. The collection includes intricate costumes, rice-wine jars, musical instruments and baskets of K'ho, Ede, Ma, Jarai, S'tieng and Bahnar. An impressive new facility is under construction behind the present museum, and will hopefully open in late 2011.

Exploring the City

A few **Ede villages** lay at the outskirts of town, such as Ako Dhong, and are worth visiting if there is still daylight. Around Ly Thuong Kiet Street are some of the only **craft shops** in Vietnam where authentic crafts of Central Highlands hill tribes can be purchased. Have dinner at one of the ***nem nuong* restaurants** in the neighborhood, see ③.

Food and Drink

② THANG LOI RESTAURANT

Thang Loi Hotel; 1 Phan Chu Trinh Street, Buon Ma Thuot; daily B, L & D; $$

Thang Loi is located on the ground floor of a hotel, overlooking Liberty Square. The menu has a good selection of international and Vietnamese cuisine. This is perhaps the best restaurant in town.

③ NEM NUONG RESTAURANTS

East side of Ly Thuong Kiet Street, between No Trang Long & Quang Truong streets; daily B, L & D; $

Nem nuong are roll-it-yourself fresh spring rolls with grilled meats, fresh herbs, pickled vegetables and boiled eggs. This strip of restaurants is conveniently located amidst the town's most popular budget accommodation.

Above from far left: Ako Dhong village, near Buon Ma Thuot; Dray Sap waterfall; ducks at market in Buon Ma Thuot.

Going further

From Buon Ma Thuot, you have a choice of continuing on to Pleiku (five hours to the north) and then Kon Tum (another two hours), or heading out to the coast north of Nha Trang (an all-day drive). All of the drives have beautiful scenery, and Kon Tum has fascinating Bahnar and Jarai villages.

8

HOI AN OLD TOWN

Hoi An, once an important port, retains its old-town atmosphere and architecture as a World Heritage Site, yet has become one of Vietnam's top shopping destinations, despite its small size. Spend your days exploring old temples, assembly halls, shrines, and ancient shop houses.

DISTANCE 4km (2½-mile) walk
TIME One busy day or two leisurely days with lots of shopping and café breaks
START Le Loi Street Ticket Office
END Quan Thang House
POINTS TO NOTE
Hoi An is best reached by plane or train to nearby Da Nang. This tour can be grouped with the Cham Holy Land tour. Hoi An is the most family-friendly destination in Vietnam, and one of the few wheelchair-friendly towns in the country. All roads are paved, and sidewalks are unusually clear of clutter.

About 25km (15 miles) southeast of Da Nang, the ancient town of **Hoi An** nestles on the banks of the **Thu Bon River**. Originally a seaport in the Champa Kingdom, by the 15th century it had become a coastal Vietnamese town under the Tran Dynasty. At the beginning of the 16th century, the Portuguese came to explore the coast of Hoi An. Then came the Chinese, Japanese, Dutch, British and French.

Hoi An appeared in Western travelogues in the 17th and 18th centuries as Faifo or Hai Po. For several centuries Hoi An was one of the most important trading ports in Southeast Asia. By the beginning of the 19th century the mouth of the Thu Bon silted up and another port was built at the mouth of the Han River. Thenceforth Da Nang replaced Hoi An as the centre of trade.

In the early 1980s, Unesco and the Polish government funded a restoration programme to classify and safeguard Hoi An's old quarters and historic monuments. Hoi An was designated a Unesco World Heritage Site in 1999.

An admission ticket of VND90,000 (sold by various tour offices around the perimeter) gains you entry to one each of four museums, four old houses, three assembly halls, the Handicraft Workshop (with traditional music concert), and either the Japanese Bridge or the Quan Cong Temple. The system is designed so that you need to purchase a total of four tickets to see everything. Most sites are open daily from 7am to 6pm and require an Old Town Ticket, unless otherwise noted.

Flooding
The town is prone to flooding during periods of heavy rains in October and November. This does not necessarily mean the Old Town will be closed. Small boats may simply ferry visitors around the streets which are flooded.

DAY 1: THE WEST SIDE AND JAPANESE QUARTER

Le Loi Street is centrally located and a good place to start your exploration. Heading south towards the river, buy your ticket at the **ticket office** ❶ on your right as you enter the Old Quarter.

Cantonese Assembly Hall and Sa Huynh Museum

Turn right on Tran Phu Street and head to the **Cantonese Assembly Hall** ❷ (Hoi Quan Quang Dong; 176 Tran Phu Street), founded in 1786. It's a pleasant spot with an amusing fountain in the middle of the courtyard, composed of a twisted dragon set to devour a carp, and a turtle spying from behind. It's all beautifully decorated in colored ceramic tiles. Large red coils of incense hang from the ceilings, hung by numerous families as offerings.

Across the street, the **Museum of Sa Huynh Culture** ❸ (Bao Tang Van Hoa; 149 Tran Phu Street; daily 8am–5pm) has a nice collection of ancient pottery and jewellery from local excavations.

Japanese Covered Bridge

One of the most remarkable architectural pieces in town is the **Japanese Covered Bridge** ❹ (Cau Nhat Ban/Lai Vien Kieu). Built by the Japanese community in the 16th century, it links the Chinese and Japanese quarters, and Tran Phu Street with Nguyen Thi Minh Khai. The bridge's curved shape and undulating green- and yellow-tiled roof give the impression of moving water. According to legend, a monster with his head in India, his tail in Japan and his heart in Hoi An was causing local calamities. The bridge was erected at the heart to kill this monster, known as 'Cu'. Tradition also states that the bridge was started in the year of the monkey and finished in the year of the dog. Thus, a stone pair of each now stands at either end of the bridge as guardians.

Above from far left: Hoi An on the banks of Thu Bon River; Japanese Covered Bridge.

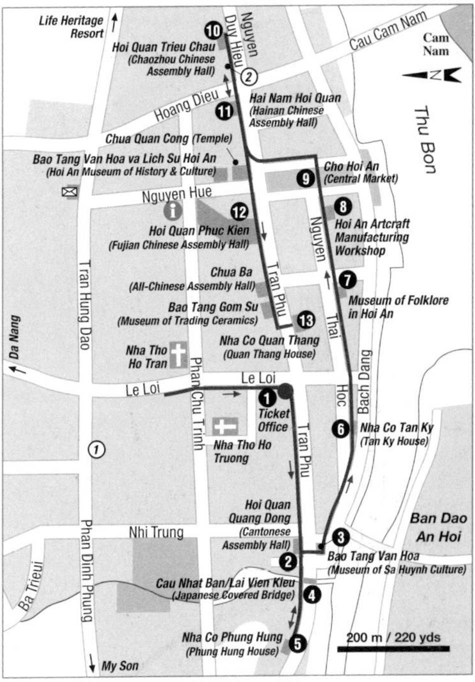

Phung Hung and Tan Ky Houses

The **Phung Hung House** ❺ (Nha Co Phung Hung; 4R Nguyen Thi Minh Khai Street; free), which has Japanese and Chinese architectural influences, is still family-owned after nearly 230 years. They give guided tours, a free tea service, have an embroidery shop in the back and a gift shop upstairs.

From here, turn back to the covered bridge and make your way to the right on Nguyen Thai Hoc Street, continuing until you reach the **Tan Ky House** ❻ (Nha Co Tan Ky; 101 Nguyen Thai Hoc Street; daily 8am–noon, 2–4.30pm). Typical of the old houses in Hoi An, it is a two-storey home built of finely decorated precious wood. An inner courtyard is open to the sky, with a veranda linking several living quarters. Although many of the old Hoi An homes have been restored over the years, they retain their original wooden framework, carved doors and windows, and sculpted stuccos, as well as very rare antiques from Vietnam, China, Japan and France. Likewise, one of the most remarkable features of these old homes is their amalgamation of these cultures within the architecture itself.

For lunch or dinner, head to **Jenny's Café and Bamboo Restaurant**, see ①, on Tran Hung Dao at the north edge of the Old Town.

Below: take a guided tour around Phung Hung House.

DAY 2: THE EAST SIDE AND FRENCH QUARTER

Start from where the previous day's tour finished off and walk west on Nguyen Thai Hoc Street.

The Museum of Folklore, Handicraft Workshop and Central Market

The **Museum of Folklore in Hoi An** ❼ (33 Nguyen Thai Hoc Street; tel: 051-091 0948; daily 8am–5pm; free) is in an old house with a craft shop downstairs and an excellent museum upstairs, featuring exhibits of artisan tools, ancient crafts and local folklore.

The **Hoi An Artcraft Manufacturing Workshop** ❽ ('Handicraft Workshop', 9 Nguyen Thai Hoc Street) is located in a 200-year-old Chinese merchant shop. Lanterns and other souvenir crafts are made and sold in the back of the shop. The main draw is the traditional music and dance show at 10.15am and 3.15pm each day.

Continue east and make your way through the **Central Market** ❾ (Cho Hoi An; free), a great place to pick up snacks and fresh fruit and to find better bargains than in most street shops.

Assembly Halls and Quan Thang House

Turn left on Hoang Dieu Street, heading northwest. Then turn right on Nguyen Duy Hieu, heading northeast to the **Chaozhou Chinese Assembly Hall** ❿ (Hoi Quan Trieu Chau, opposite 157 Nguyen Duy Hieu Street; daily 8am–5pm), built in 1776. The altars are some of the finest examples of wood-carving motifs in Hoi An. The roofs of the structure are decorated with elaborate miniature figures of soldiers, deities, dragons and mythical beasts, all composed of colourful ceramic tiles.

Backtracking on Nguyen Duy Hieu, consider a refreshment stop at **Moon Restaurant**, see ②, before the street becomes Tran Phu. The **Hainan Chinese Assembly Hall** ⓫ (Hai Nam Hoi Quan; 10 Tran Phu Street; daily 8am–5pm; free) was built in 1851 and is a memorial to 107 Chinese merchants who were murdered by a rogue commanding officer in Emperor Tu Duc's navy. Ton That Thieu had looted the ships and claimed that pirates were responsible, but his crimes were later discovered and he was gruesomely executed along with his officers.

Continue on Tran Phu Street to the **Fujian Chinese Assembly Hall** ⓬ (Hoi Quan Phuc Kien; across from 35 Tran Phu Street). The largest and most elaborate of the assembly halls in town, it was turned into a temple to Thien Hau and houses idols of numerous Chinese deities. Worshippers believe Thien Hau rescues sailors from sinking ships.

Finally, the **Quan Thang House** ⓭ (77 Tran Phu Street) is more than 300 years old and has been in the current family for six generations. It is sparsely decorated with two family altars and a small courtyard.

Food and Drink

① JENNY'S CAFÉ AND BAMBOO RESTAURANT

15 Tran Huong Dao Street; daily B, L & D; $$

This popular eatery specialises in local Hoi An cuisine, with other Vietnamese and backpacker favourites like pizza, pasta, burgers and sandwiches also on the menu. Try their addictive fried wontons topped with sweet and sour shrimp stir-fry.

② MOON RESTAURANT & LOUNGE

321 Nguyen Duy Hieu; tel: 0510-324 1396; www.hoianmoonrestaurant.com; daily B, L & D; $$

Service is very friendly at this 'classical Vietnamese restaurant with a modern twist', set in an old French colonial building with wooden interiors and decorated with a gallery of paintings. It has a cosy atmosphere and a nice bar.

Above from far left: Tan Ky House; Chaozhou Chinese Assembly Hall; inside Phung Hung House.

Magical wells

Within the Old Town is a network of 1,000-year-Old Wells, constructed by the Cham. The wells are attributed with magical properties, and it is said only their water may be used to make the local dish, *cao lau*.

9

CHAM HOLY LAND

Take a day or two's drive through some beautiful coastal scenery and Vietnam's third-largest city of Da Nang on your way to visiting the holiest sites and relics of the ancient Champa Kingdom.

DISTANCE 93km (58 miles)
TIME A long day by car, or two day trips
START Museum of Cham Sculpture, Da Nang
END The Cargo Club, Hoi An
POINTS TO NOTE
Da Nang is best reached by train from Hue, or by air from Cam Ranh near Nha Trang. This tour can be grouped with tour 8. This tour is generally suitable for the whole family. My Son requires a lot of walking, and visitors must stay on marked paths. Landmines may still exist off the beaten path, so take care and stick to the beaten ones.

The Champa Kingdom once occupied the area of Da Nang, Hoi An and Quang Nam Province, known collectively as Amaravati, for a thousand years. While most of the Cham were pushed south to Binh Thuan and Ninh Thuan provinces (the Cham province of Panduranga), remnant tribes of the ancient multiethnic kingdom still live in the area. The Cham holy city of My Son and the Da Nang Museum of Cham Sculpture together form one of the greatest collections of Champa art and architecture. The Marble Mountains, which once housed Cham shrines, makes a pleasant interlude.

Have breakfast before you start or brunch after the museum, at the superb **Bread of Life**, see 🍴①, at the Bach Dang and Dong Da roundabout. Afterwards, drive south on Tran Phu Street until it terminates at the museum.

Local marble
Marble from here was used in the construction of Ho Chi Minh's tomb in Hanoi, a fact the locals are fiercely proud of. The mountains were also a haven for the Viet Cong during the war as they overlooked the vast air force base used by the Americans.

THE MUSEUM OF CHAM SCULPTURE

Begin your tour at Da Nang's **Museum of Cham Sculpture ❶** (Bao Tang Dieu Khac Champa; Number 2, 2 Thang 9 Street; daily 8am–5pm; charge). This extensive collection of superbly preserved statuary was established in 1915 by the École Française d'Extrême-Orient (EFEO). Buy the useful booklet (*Museum of Cham Culture – Danang*, Foreign Languages Publishing House, Hanoi, 1987) written by the museum curator, Tran Ky Phuong, on sale at the entrance.

You will walk through rooms featuring four different periods (displayed somewhat haphazardly) dating from the seventh to the 15th century, according to their city of origin: My Son, Tra Kieu, Dong Duong and Thap Mam. The wealth of Hindu relics removed from My Son and neighbouring Tra Kieu represent some of the finest examples of Cham art. Dong Duong was a Buddhist enclave in the Champa Kingdom, also found in Quang Nam Province. Thap Mam, located far south in Quy Nhon, represents the decline of Champa, when the art had become rather stylised.

The museum contains the largest display of Cham artefacts in the world. At the centre of the museum you will see the deity Ganesh with his elephant head, recurring examples of Shiva dancing in his warlike manner, Nandin the bull mount of Shiva and many other figures, all sensuously erotic and finely carved.

THE MARBLE MOUNTAINS

Take any of the bridges east across the Han River, then drive south on either coastal road to the **Marble Mountains** ❷ (Ngu Hanh Son). Each is named for one of the five Daoist phases of Wu Xing: Kim Son (metal), Thuy Son (water), Moc Son (wood), Hoa Son (fire) and Tho Son (earth). Caves within the mountains were once used by Cham and now shelter altars dedicated to Buddha,

Above from far left: Museum of Cham Sculpture, Da Nang; Marble Mountains.

Food and Drink

① BREAD OF LIFE

Dong Da Street at Bach Dang Street Roundabout; tel: 0511-356 5185; www.breadoflifedanang.com; daily B, L & D; $$

This bakery, wifi café and restaurant, serving authentic American comfort food, is staffed almost entirely by the deaf. The menu includes pizza, pasta, burgers, sandwiches, elaborate breakfasts and baked macaroni. Expats come from hours away for special holiday meals.

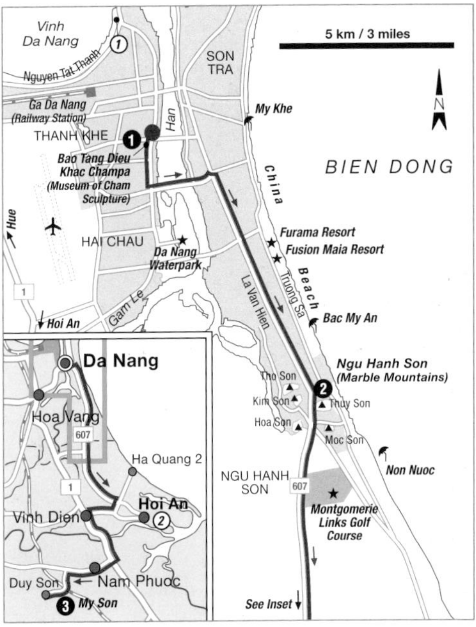

Champa temples
The temples of Champa generally followed one basic, three-storey design. They represent Mount Meru, the Hindu abode of the gods, and generally face east towards the rising sun. The inner sanctum normally had a Shivalinga at its centre.

various bodhisattvas and the local deities worshipped by the area's inhabitants.

The most famous mountain, which is riddles with caves, temples and paths, is **Thuy Son** (daily 7am–5pm; charge). The paths weaving through the mountain are well marked and easy to navigate. The largest mountain, Thuy Son, is home to several caves, some of which were used as Buddhist sanctuaries and even as a Viet Cong hospital. Take the second entrance on your left as you walk towards the beach. **Huyen Khong Cave** – a Buddhist sanctuary which served as a Viet Cong base – is the most spectacular. The highest cave, **Van Thong**, has a narrow passage through which you can wiggle to the top for the breathtaking views.

Below: souvenirs crafted from the Marble Mountains.

MY SON

Take road 607 south towards Hoi An, then turn west on road 608 towards Highway 1A. Travelling south from Hoi A on Highway 1A for 27km (16 miles), turn right after entering Nam Phuoc village, at the sign for My Son. Fork left after 9km (5½ miles). This journey should take less than an hour. Buy your ticket at the mini museum and reception hall and then ride the shuttle bus about 1km (⅔ mile) to the start of the path.

The valley of **My Son** ❸ (tel: 0510-373 1757; 7am–5pm; charge), nestled under Cat's Tooth Mountain, was chosen as a religious sanctuary by King Bhadravarman I, and from the fourth century, many temples and towers *(kalan)* were built in this area. These ruins are all that remains of the ancient religious capital of Amaravati, the greatest of the Cham states.

The Cham people worshipped a dual cosmology, venerating both male and female deities. In Amaravati, My Son represented the male god king, denoted by the holy Cat's Tooth Mountain and a phallic representation, the *linga* Bhadresvarain. 'Bhad' is an abbreviation of Bhadravarman, and 'esvara' refers to the Hindu god Shiva.

During the Second Indochina War (1954–75), the Viet Cong based

themselves in the temples, using them as bunkers. American B52s bombed them thoroughly, leaving only a small vestige of what was once a magnificent ancient city. Traces of around 70 temples and related structures may still be found at My Son, though only about 20 are still in good condition.

Walking in a uni-directional loop, you will encounter designated temple groups: A, A', B, C, D, E and F. The additional groups, H, L and G are off-limits. The first cluster of temples which you encounter at **groups C, B and D** are the most intact, but the others are in various states of cataclysmic collapse. Two **meditation halls** *(mandapa)* in D have been turned into small galleries containing modest examples of sculpture, although the most interesting pieces have been carted off to other museums. Stone phallic symbols abound throughout the temples, in the form of the male *linga* and female *yoni*. Worshipped as a symbol of the god Shiva, sacred water was poured over the *linga* and drained through the *yoni*.

After a long afternoon turn back towards Hoi An, turning east from Highway 1A on road 608, then following the river into town. Once back in Hoi An, head to the Japanese Bridge and have dinner at **The Cargo Club**, see 🍴②.

Above from far left: Huyen Khong Cave; temple group B at My Son; Cham woman at Po Nagar Cham towers.

Food and Drink

② THE CARGO CLUB RESTAURANT AND HOI AN PATISSERIE

107–109 Nguyen Thai Hoc Street; tel: 0510-391 1227; www.hoianhospitality.com; daily B, L & D; $$$

The food at Hoi An's Cargo Club is a cut above its neighbours. The menu includes international fare, French pastries, home-made ice cream and a well-stocked wine bar.

Ancient Champa

The Kingdom of Champa may have been established around the second century, and for about 1,000 years (5th–15th century) it flourished in this region of Vietnam. At its apogee, Champa controlled the entire central coast of what would later become Vietnam, from the Hoanh Son Pass in the north to Vung Tau in the south. Their country functioned as a loose confederation of five states named after regions of India –Indrapura (Quang Tri), Amaravati (Quang Nam), Vijaya (Binh Dinh), Kauthara (Nha Trang) and Panduranga (Phan Rang).

At the start of the 10th century, Champa came under severe pressure from Dai Viet, which was beginning its long push to the south. In 1069, Indrapura was lost to the Viets, and by 1306, Champa's northern frontier had been pushed back to the Hai Van Pass with the loss of Amaravati. The process of Vietnamese expansion proved inexorable, with Vijaya falling in 1471 and Champa – now reduced to the kingdoms of Kauthara and Panduranga – effectively a broken power. The final absorption by Vietnam was delayed until the reign of Minh Mang in 1832.

Champa disappeared – but not the Cham people. Some fled to neighbouring Cambodia, though others chose to stay under Vietnamese tutelage in their southern homelands.

10

HUE'S IMPERIAL CITY

The home of the Nguyen kings, Hue's Imperial City was the seat of Vietnam's last royal dynasty. Walk through the king's gardens, royal temples and palace halls to experience at first hand the grandeur of the Nguyen Royal Court.

DISTANCE 1.5km (1-mile) walk
TIME A half-day
START Trang Tien Bridge on the Perfume River
END Hue Historical and Revolutionary Museum
POINTS TO NOTE
Hue is best reached from Hanoi or Da Nang by train. Transport to and from the citadel is most convenient by taxi. This tour is best grouped with tour 11. Bring an umbrella unless there is a good reason to think it won't rain. Hue is one of the rainiest cities in Vietnam. Plan to eat before or after the tour. There are no restaurants once inside the Ngo Mon. Time the tour to take in one of the 30-minute shows (9.30am, 10.30am, 2.30pm and 3.30pm) at the Royal Theatre.

Guided tours
The optional guides (charge) from the Hue Monument Conservation Centre, located at the Ngo Mon, speak reasonably good English (other languages available) and are knowledgeable.

In 1802, after quelling the Tay Son rebellion, Lord Nguyen Phuc Anh proclaimed himself Emperor Gia Long and founded the Nguyen Dynasty. He ordered the new royal citadel to be built along the Perfume River, which became Vietnam's new capital city. Just 33 years into the dynasty's reign, the French invaded Hue. They retained the Nguyen Dynasty with nominal governance over central Vietnam and northern Vietnam. Thanks to French manipulation of the dynasty, a quick succession of emperors graced the throne, ending with Bao Dai's abdication in 1945.

ENTERING THE CITADEL

Grab a bite at **La Boulangerie Française**, see 🍴①, before heading north, crossing the Perfume River via **Trang Tien Bridge** ❶. Enter the citadel on the north bank. Hue's **Imperial City** (Dai Noi), including the Yellow Enclosure and Forbidden Purple City (Tu Cam Thanh), is enclosed within the all-encompassing *Kinh Thanh* (the exterior enclosure). Stone, bricks and earth were used for this wall, which was 8m (26ft) high and 20m (65ft) thick. Ten large, fortified gates, each topped with watchtowers, were built along the wall. Most of what visitors come to see today is within the Yellow Enclosure; other areas were destroyed

during the Tet Offensive of 1968.

Immediately inside the first enclosure of the royal city, towards the Chuong Duc gate, are the **Nine Deities' Cannons** ❷ (Sung Than Cong). The five cannons on one side represent the five elements – metal, water, wood, fire, and earth – while the other four represent the seasons.

The **Yellow Enclosure** (Hoang Thanh; daily 7am–5.30pm; charge) is the middle wall enclosing the Imperial City and its palaces, temples and flower gardens. Four richly decorated gates provided access: Ngo Mon (the southern gate, or Noon Gate), Hoa Binh (northern gate), Hien Nhon (eastern gate) and Chuong Duc (western gate).

THE NGO MON

You will enter the Imperial City through the **Ngo Mon** ❸ (Noon Gate) was built of granite in 1834 during the reign of Minh Mang and is the most recognisable structure in the city. It is topped by the **Five Phoenix Watchtower** (Lau Ngu Phung).

From here, the emperors used to preside over formal ceremonies, including Emperor Bao Dai's abdication.The gate is also known as the 'Noon Gate' because the sun, representing the emperor, is at its highest at noon. It faces south and is also therefore associated with prosperity. Purchase your tickets for the citadel here.

THAI HOA PALACE

Through the Ngo Mon, walk across the Golden Water Bridge, which at one time was reserved for the emperor. It leads to **Thai Hoa Palace** ❹ (Dien Thai Hoa) or 'Palace of Supreme Harmony', the most important administrative structure in the Imperial City. Here the emperor held bimonthly audiences with the court, including male members of

Above from far left: Trag Tien Bridge; cyclos passing by Ngo Mon.

Food and Drink

① LA BOULANGERIE FRANÇAISE

41 Nguyen Tri Phuong; tel: 054-383 7437; daily B, L & D; $

The Boulangerie is the finest French bakery in Vietnam. The tarts, cakes and breads look great and taste better. It also does excellent work by training disadvantaged street kids as bakers and pastry chefs.

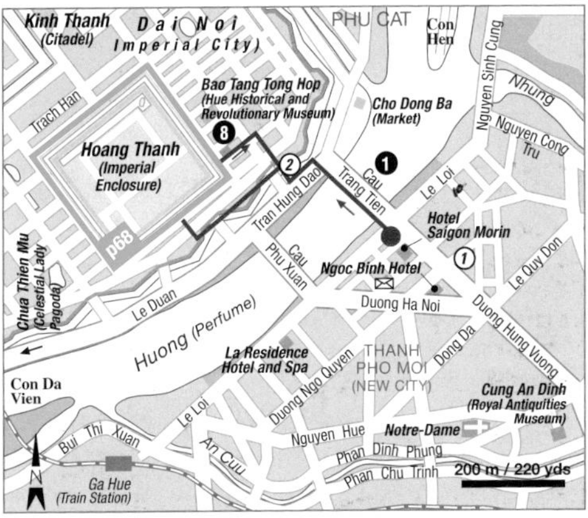

Royal Theatre tickets
The de luxe ticket (double price) at the Royal Theatre includes a cup of tea and a biscuit, perhaps enhancing the atmosphere during the show, but not a good value.

the royal family, with civil mandarins standing before him on the left, and military mandarins on the right. The palace is in excellent condition, with its ceilings and 80 gilded beams decorated in red lacquer and gold inlay.

THE FORBIDDEN PURPLE CITY

Walking north through Thai Hoa, the **Forbidden Purple City** (Tu Cam Thanh) was reserved solely for the emperor and the royal family, who resided here behind a brick wall 4m (13ft) thick. This area was almost completely destroyed during the Tet Offensive of 1968 (the Viet Cong used the citadel as a bunker) and nearly everything that was left after that succumbed to flooding and neglect in tropical conditions.

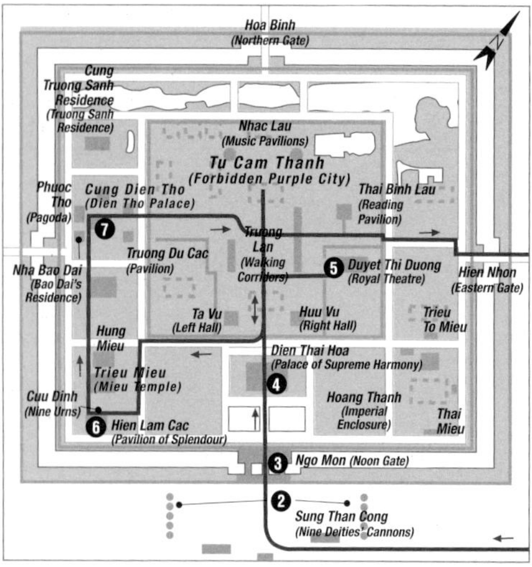

The Mandarin Halls

When you first enter the area you'll find the **Left and Right Halls of the Mandarins**. The Left Hall is now devoted to photo opportunities in period costumes (charge), and the Right Hall houses an extension of the **Royal Antiquities Museum**, with small exhibits of silver, bronze, wood and writing crafts from the Nguyen Dynasty.

The Royal Theatre and Reading Pavilion

The **Royal Theatre** ❺ (Duyet Thi Duong), behind and to the right (east), offers 30-minute shows in the morning at 9.30 and 10.30am, and afternoons at 2.30 and 3.30pm. Performances include five or six songs and dances in elaborate customs (including lion dancers).

Food and Drink

② LAC THIEN, LAC THANH AND LAC THUAN
06 Dinh Tien Hoang; tel: 054-352 7348; daily B, L & D; $
This strip of three eateries owned by deaf siblings opened in 1965 and are the most famous in the city, partly due to their appearance in the *Globetrekker* TV series. They are known for giving customers their trademark wooden bottle-openers as souvenirs.

Above from far left: Thai Hoa Palace; Halls of the Mandarins; the Nine Dynastic Urns.

The emperor's **Reading Pavilion** sits behind the theatre, ornately decorated with tiles, although it looks like it could collapse at any time. A number of new **covered walking corridors** have been recreated in the central field, taking significant artistic licence. In the far reaches of the expanse behind them is a pair of octagonal **Music Pavilions**.

THE TEMPLES

Return to the Thai Hoa Palace and walk west along the path to the next enclosure. The temple-shrines *(mieu)* here are dedicated to worshipping various lords and royal family members. The temple of **Trieu To Mieu** is devoted to Nguyen Kim (now used as a plant nursery), the **Thai Mieu** to Nguyen Hoang and his successors, and **Phung Tien** is a temple established to worship all of the emperors of the reigning dynasty, the **To Mieu** complex houses numerous shrines of significance as well. **Hung Mieu** is on the north side of the complex and devoted to Nguyen Phuc Luan, Gia Long's father. The well-preserved **The Mieu** houses the shrines of nine Nguyen emperors.

The Pavilion of Splendour

Also in the To Mieu complex, in front of The Mieu temple, stands the magnificently restored **Hien Lam Cac** ❻ (Pavilion of Splendour), with the **Nine Dynastic Urns** (Cuu Dinh) lined up before it *(see margin tip, right)*.

DIEN THO PALACE

Following the signs north, the **Dien Tho Palace** ❼, built in 1804, was the traditional residence of queen mothers. It includes a bewildering 20 structures, most notably the **Phuoc Tho Pagoda**, the recent **Personal Residence of Emperor Bao Dai**, and the lovely **Truong Du Pavilion**, nestled against a small lotus pond. The beauty of the complex rivals Thai Hoa Palace.

The **Truong Sanh Residence** is a separate complex behind the palace and served as a recreation area for the queen mother.

HUE HISTORICAL AND REVOLUTIONARY MUSEUM

Exit through Hien Nhon (the eastern gate) to the nearby **Hue Historical and Revolutionary Museum** ❽ (Bao Tang Tong Hop; Tue–Sun 7.30–11am, 1.30–5pm; free). The central building, built in the style of a traditional *dinh* (communal house), contains a collection of local archaeological discoveries. The colonial pavilions outside are devoted to the First and Second Indochina Wars.

End the royal tour by sampling a wide selection of unique dishes at the strip of three family-run restaurants known as **Lac Thien, Lac Thanh** and **Lac Thuan**, see Ⓡ②, which can be found on the south side of the citadel.

The Nine Dynastic Urns

Hundreds of artisans from all over the country were involved in the casting of these urns. Each one represents an emperor of the Nguyen Dynasty and weighs up to 2,500kg (5,600lbs). The urns, cast between 1835 and 1837 during Minh Mang's reign, are decorated with motifs of the sun, moon, birds, animals, dragons, mountains, rivers, historic events, and scenes from everyday life.

11

TOMBS OF THE NGUYEN DYNASTY

Some were loved and others hated, but all the kings of Vietnam's last ruling family live on in infamy. Spend a day wandering among the monuments, gardens, lakes and chapels of the Nguyen emperors.

DISTANCE 32km (20 miles)
TIME A full day
START Tu Duc's Tomb
END Nam Giao Dan
POINTS TO NOTE
Plan to eat before or after the tour, or else buy a picnic lunch from La Boulangerie Française (see tour 10). This tour may be completed by a combination of car, motorbike or bicycle, and boat.

The tombs of the Nguyen kings lie scattered on the hillsides along either side of the Perfume River, to the west and south of Hue. Although the dynasty had 13 kings, only seven of them reigned until their deaths, and only they are laid to rest in this valley of kings: Gia Long, Minh Mang, Thieu Tri, Tu Duc, Kien Phuc, Dong Khanh and Khai Dinh. Roads are marked with signs to the tombs, but infrequently, and they are written entirely in Vietnamese. There's no one correct way to see the tombs, so if you choose to see most of them, it may require some backtracking.

Tu Duc's Tomb

Follow Bui Thi Xuan West along the Perfume River turning left (south) at the sign for the imperial tombs. The **tomb of Tu Duc** ❶ is the first you will encounter, and surrounded by an onslaught of incense and souvenir shops. The mausoleum construction, begun in 1864, took three years to complete. The result resembles a royal palace in miniature and harmonises beautifully with the natural surroundings. It is perhaps the loveliest of all the Nguyen tombs and the most visited. Live traditional music is periodically performed within the tomb grounds each day for the benefit of visitors.

Tu Duc, the son of Thieu Tri and the Nguyen Dynasty's fourth king, reigned for 36 years, the longest reign of any of the Nguyen kings. He spent his leisure hours in the two pavilions beside the lake, Luu Khiem, where he wrote poetry, no doubt inspired by the beauty of his surroundings, and often went fishing. Xung Khiem is the more interesting of the two lakeside pavilions. A staircase leads to the Luong Khiem mausoleum, which contains a

Stay scam-safe
Beware of friendly people who pull up beside you on motorbikes, offering to show you the way to tombs and temples outside the royal city because its 'on the way home to their village'. Several scams start this way.

collection of furniture, vases and jewellery boxes. Further on is the terrace leading to the tomb, with its stone elephants, horses and mandarins. The tomb itself, ritually inaccessible, is covered by dense pine forest. The tombs of Tu Duc's adopted son, Kien Phu, and Queen Le Thien An, lie beside the lake.

Thieu Tri's Tomb

The **tomb of Thieu Tri** ❷ (daylight hours; free) is located a few kilometres to the south along the Perfume River. Thieu Tri, Minh Mang's son, was the third Nguyen emperor and reigned from 1841–7. His tomb was built in the same elegant architectural style as his father's but on a much smaller scale, and is now crumbling. The mausoleum sprawls across several lakes and is largely open, without the surrounding walls found around other tombs.

Minh Mang's Tomb

The **tomb of Minh Mang** ❸ (daily 8am–5pm; charge) is located about 5km (3 miles) south, where the Ta Trach and Huu Trach tributaries of thePerfume River meet. Turn left (east) at the overpass and take the bridge across the river.

Minh Mang was Gia Long's fourth son and the Nguyen Dynasty's second king. Construction of the tomb was begun a year before Minh Mang's death in 1840, and was finished by his successor Thieu Tri in 1843. The setting blends the beauty of nature with the majestic architecture and superb stone sculpture created by its many anonymous craftsmen. It is at its best in mid-March, when the Trung Minh and Tan Nguyet lakes bloom with a mass of beautiful lotus flowers.

Now would be a good time to break for a picnic lunch or head back into Hue and resume the rest of the tour tomorrow.

Gia Long's Tomb

The **tomb of Gia Long** ❹ (daily 8am–5pm; charge) is located 16km

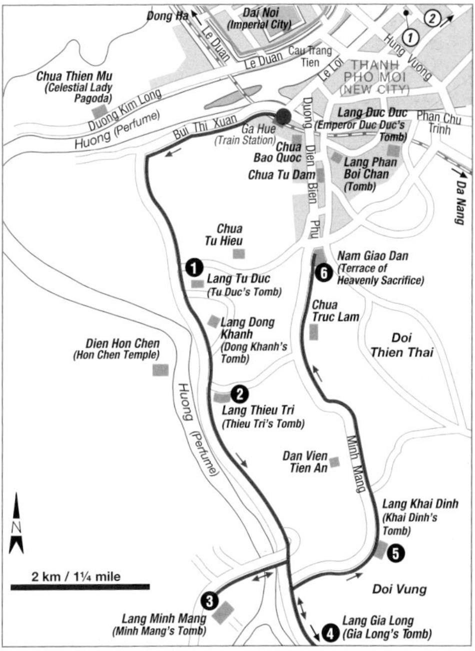

Above:
stone statues at the tomb of Khai Dinh.

Divisive figure
Minh Mang was responsible for the construction of the Imperial City of Hue. He was highly respected by the Vietnamese for his reforms in the areas of customs, traditions and agriculture. However, he is disliked to this day by the Cham, as the Vietnamese ruler who dealt the last blow to the declining Champa Kingdom.

Below:
Minh Mang's tomb.

(10 miles) south from Hue. To get there from Minh Mang's tomb, cross back over to the east side of the river, head south for at least 1km (⅔ mile), and stop at the nearest boat landing to be ferried across to the tomb. The tomb sits on a hillside, and is inaccessible by road. The tomb, begun in 1814, was completed a year after Gia Long's death in 1820. Unfortunately, the site was in the middle of a guerrilla zone during the Vietnam War, and the tomb was considerably damaged by bombs. The tomb has been rather neglected, but the wild beauty of the site itself, with its mountainous backdrop, makes the effort to get there well worth the time.

Khai Dinh's Tomb

About 3km (2 miles) back across the river and north on Road 49, the **tomb of Khai Dinh** ❺ (daily 8am–5pm; charge) somewhat resembles a European castle, its architecture a blend of the oriental and occidental. Made of reinforced concrete, it took 11 years to complete and was finally finished in 1931. Khai Dinh, Bao Dai's adopted father, ruled for nine years during the colonial era. A grandiose dragon staircase leads up to the first courtyard, from where further stairs lead to a courtyard lined with stone statues of elephants, horses, and civil and military mandarins. In the centre of the courtyard stands the stele inscribed with Chinese characters

composed by Bao Dai in memory of his father. The exterior lacks the tranquil charm and beauty of Minh Mang's or Tu Duc's mausoleum, and the giant dragons flanking the staircase appear rather menacing.

Once inside, however, the contrast is striking and more identifiable with the ostentatious character of the emperor. Coloured tiles pave the floor, and a huge 'dragon in the clouds' mural, painted by artists using their feet, adorns the ceiling of the middle chamber. Jade-green antechambers lead off to the left and right. Bright frescoes composed of many thousands of inlaid ceramic and glass fragments depict various themes. Animals, trees and flowers provide a visual feast after the morbid, blackened exterior of the mausoleum. The back room contains a small museum of the emperor's possessions, including photos, clothing, ceramics, crystal, furniture and a clock. A life-size bronze statue of Khai Dinh, made in France in 1922, rests on a dais on top of the tomb.

Nam Giao Dan

Head about 4km (2½ miles) south on Dien Bien Phu (also known as Minh Mang Street or road 49 here) to **Nam Giao Dan** ❻ (Terrace of Heavenly Sacrifice; daylight hours recommended; free), an esplanade surrounded by a park of pines and conifers. Built by Gia Long in 1802, in its day it was considered a very sacred and solemn place. Composed of three terraces – two square and one circular – the esplanade represents the union of sky and earth. Every three years the Nam Giao (Festival of Sacrifice) took place at the centre of the circular platform. From here the emperor, worshipped as a god himself, would have a buffalo sacrificed to the god of the sky, who is believed to govern the destiny of the world.

With today's tour finished, head north 2km (1¼ miles) on Dien Bien Phu, then right on Le Loi to Hue's commercial centre for dinner at **La Carambole**, see 🍴①, or **Tropical Garden**, see 🍴②.

Food and Drink

① LA CARAMBOLE

19 Pham Ngu Lao; tel: 054-381 0491; daily B, L & D; $$$

La Carambole has a festive atmosphere with a packed house in the evenings. The menu includes English, French and Vietnamese favourites. Try the quiche and the home-made lemon sorbet. The staff's English is good and the service is fast.

② TROPICAL GARDEN

27 Chu Van An; tel: 054-384 7143; daily B, L & D; $$$

Tropical Garden serves traditional Hue cuisine with a traditional four-piece orchestra from 6–9pm nightly. Try the set menus or just come for ice cream and music. Sit in the garden by the street or inside the bamboo enclosure.

Above from far left: dragon staircase in front of Khai Dinh's tomb; the tomb of Minh Mang.

Above: stone mandarin and detail at the tomb of Tu Duc.

12

HANOI: ART AND ARCHITECTURE

The political and cultural capital of Vietnam, Hanoi is one of Asia's loveliest cities, with tree-lined, history-drenched boulevards. Stroll around Vietnam's famous urban lake, explore the 1,000-year-old Merchants' Quarter, delight in French Colonial architecture and browse the nation's best museums.

DISTANCE Day 1: walk 5km (3½ miles), drive 4km (2½ miles); Day 2: walk 3km (2 miles), drive: 12km (7½ miles)
TIME 2 days
START Day 1: Monument to Le Thai To; Day 2: Temple of Literature
END Day 1: National Museum of Vietnamese History; Day 2: Vietnam Museum of Ethnology
POINTS TO NOTE
This tour can be combined with the tour 13, and is suitable for the whole family. Many attractions and services close at lunchtime, and several museums close on Mondays.

A changing market
Originally, a tributary ran parallel to Hang Buom (Sails Street), enabling boats to sail up here to buy nautical supplies. When the French filled in the To Lich River, merchants switched to selling imported goods and dried foodstuffs, still sold today.

Hanoi's development may lag behind other Asian capitals, but this is good news for most visitors. Despite increasingly evident development, the city still retains its unique identity, with a collection of legend-strewn lakes, low-rise colonial buildings and ancient pagodas – rather than glittering skyscrapers and shopping malls – dominating the city centre.

Downtown Hanoi, which contains Hanoi's main areas of interest, is relatively small, with a distinct provincial feel. This makes travelling around the city relatively easy. There are many interesting must-sees, but Hanoi's main draw is its ambience and street life, a drama that unfolds daily on the streets, and in temples and markets. The best way to appreciate this mesmerising city is on foot. Take your time to savour its captivating sights, absorbing the sounds and aromas found at every corner you take.

HOAN KIEM LAKE

Begin your tour at 8am; breakfast is taken en route. Your starting point is the north end of Le Thai To Street, at the northwest tip of **Hoan Kiem Lake**. Head south down Le Thai To Street. To your right, inside the **Monument to Le Thai To** ❶ is a statue of Emperor Le Thai To and to your

left, on an islet in the lake, the three-tiered, 18th-century **Turtle Tower** ❷ (Thap Rua). At the southern end of Le Thai To Street, stop for breakfast at the **Hapro open-air lakeside café**, see 🍴①, *p.77*.

As you continue your walk, you will pass the small tower called **Hoa Phuong** opposite the **General Post Office** (Buu Dien Ha Noi). The tower was once an entrance to a pagoda. Around the southern tip of

Above from far left: General Post Office on the shore of Hoam Kiem Lake; Rising Sun Bridge.

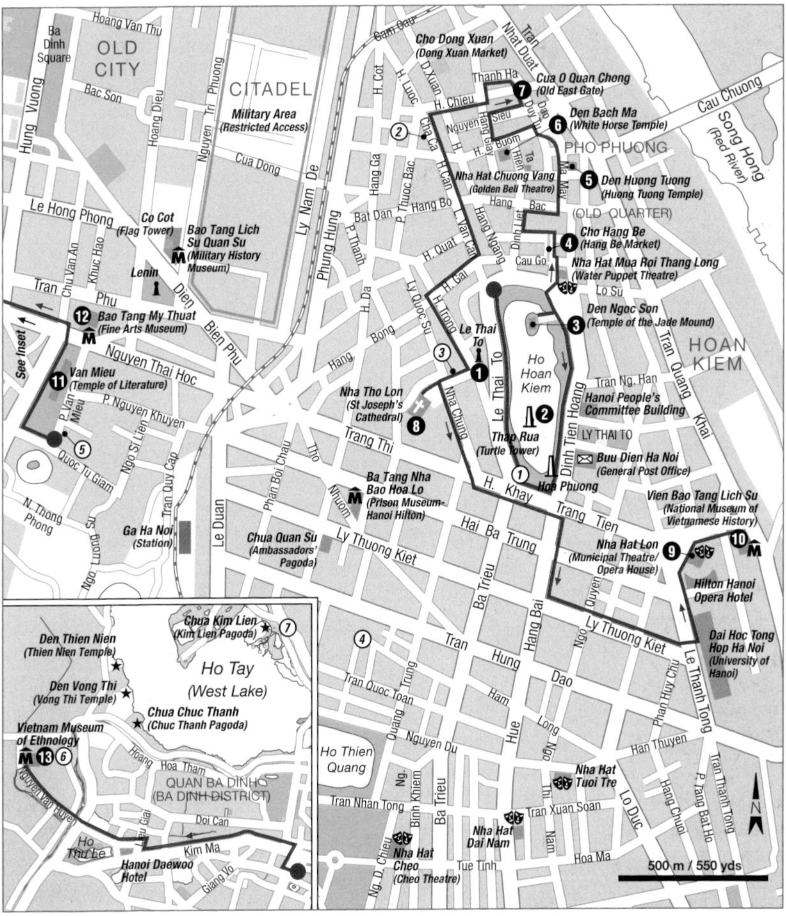

the lake, **Ly Thai To Gardens** featured a giant statue of the former emperor of the same name.

The austere, Soviet-style **Hanoi People's Committee Building** (to the right) stands in sharp contrast to the delicately arched, red-lacquered wooden **Rising Sun Bridge** (The Huc), leading to the **Ngoc Son Temple** ❸ (Den Ngoc Son), also known as the 'Temple of the Jade Mound' (daily 8am–6pm; charge). The temple is mainly associated with Tran Hung Dao, the general who defeated the Mongols at the Bach Dang River in 1279. The temple was part of a 15th-century complex of palaces, pagodas and temples, dedicated to national heroes. What remains today are mostly 19th-century buildings, one displaying a preserved giant turtle that lived in the lake. A live Hoan Kiem Lake Turtle *(Rafetus leloii)* was spotted in the lake as recently as January 2011, photographed by celebrity chef Bobby Chinn.

HANOI'S OLD QUARTER

Walk north up **Ho Hoan Kiem Street** to get to Cau Go Street. Across the road is **Hang Be Market** ❹. This is a good place to get street-food snacks, like Hanoi's famous sweet black beans and yogurt. Walk through the market, turn left and exit on **Dinh Liet Street** – the start of Hanoi's most famous sight, the Old Quarter.

The **Old Quarter** (Pho Phuong) is an ancient merchants' quarter which evolved in the 13th century when 36 artisans' guilds concentrated around the Citadel to serve the court. Each of the 36 streets was named according to the merchandise on offer, for example,

Hoan Kiem Lake

The Lake of the Restored Sword (Ho Hoan Kiem) is steeped in legend. In the 15th century, Emperor Le Thai To was supposedly handed a magic sword by a divine turtle living in the lake, helping him repel Chinese invaders. After the country had been liberated, the turtle snatched back the sword and disappeared into the lake – hence the name. This same, highly endangered species of turtle lives in the lake. Hoan Kiem was once part of the Red River and a deep swamp, the surrounding area comprising marshland and small lakes, ringed with stilt houses and dotted with small islands, until the French drained the land in the 19th century.

Hang (merchandise) or *Buom* (sails). Today, many streets have changed their wares, but some still specialise in the original craft.

Walk along Dinh Liet and turn right into Hang Bac, one of Hanoi's oldest streets. *Bac* means silver, and silversmiths originally settled here casting silver bars and coins. Today, shops still sell silver. At the intersection with Dinh Liet and Ta Hien streets, the **Golden Bell Theatre** (Nha Hat Chuong Vang) – a traditional Vietnamese theatre – was once the Hanoi Imperial Guards' headquarters.

At the end of Hang Bac, gravestone workshops spill out onto the pavements. Head into **Ma May** (Rattan Street). Members of the notorious Chinese Black Flag Army – peasant mercenaries from southern China – once lived here. In the 19th century, they helped the Vietnamese fight wars against various clans and the French.

The Old Quarter's most noteworthy antique house is **No. 87**. This former Communal House (Gioi Thieu Nha Co So), beautifully restored to its late 19th-century condition, is open to the public (daily 8.30am–5.30pm; charge). The restored **No. 69**, now transformed into the **69 Bar-Restaurant**, once had a secret tunnel used by resistance fighters running through its walls. Don't miss **Huong Tuong Temple** ❺ (Den Huong Tuong) at No. 64, founded in 1450 (open on festival days and 1st and 15th days of the lunar month; 9–11am, 3–7pm; free).

Food and Drink

① HAPRO CAFÉ

38-40 Le Thai To Street; tel: 04-3828 7043; daily B, L & D; $$

Hapro is a small alfresco café with a prime location on the banks of Hoan Kiem Lake under leafy boughs. The light menu offers coffees, juices, ice creams, plus sandwiches and breakfast. The ambience is the main draw.

White Horse Temple ❻ (Den Bach Ma), at No. 76 Hang Buom Street, is the Old Quarter's most revered and ancient place of worship, its architecture influenced by the Chinese community (daily 8–11am, 2–5pm). Founded in 1010 and restored many times, this stunning temple honours the white horse that appeared to Emperor Ly Thai To in a dream. For several decades this National Heritage Site doubled as a storage house and printing workshop. During the fight for independence from French rule, many resistance fighters hid in the temple.

Turn right into **Hang Giay** (Paper Street) – with dilapidated buildings crammed with goods – and into **Nguyen Sieu Street**. Hanoi's first inhabitants settled along the banks of the To Lich River, which flowed where this street now runs. **Co Luong Temple** (Den Co Luong) is at No. 28, its entrance flanked by two colourful guards.

Above from far left: Hang Ma Street in the Old Quarter; the Old Quarter's array of food and craft shops.

Chinese Hanoi

Many Chinese merchants settled into the Old Quarter in the 17th century and this soon became Hanoi's most affluent area, as the Chinese monopolised local commerce. To some extent they still do.

Above: in front of St Joseph's Cathedral, two practices inspire a loyal following – Catholicism and football.

Now pass along **Dao Duy Tu Street**, with its row of old houses, to reach **Old East Gate** ❼ (Cua O Quan Chong) – the only city gate to remain from the original 16 that once marked the city's entry points. To your left is **Thanh Ha Street**, a fascinating alley lined with market and food stalls. Follow it round, until you reach **Hang Chieu** (Mat Street), which turns into **Hang Ma** (Paper Votive Street) – a mass of red, with lanterns and paper votive offerings used for Buddhist ceremonies. Turn south down Cha Ca Street, stopping at No. 14 for lunch at **Cha Ca La Vong**, see ⑪②.

THE FRENCH QUARTER

Grab a taxi, cyclo, moto driver or simply walk south on Cha Ca Street, then right on Hang Gai for a shopping diversion in the boutique shops, continued with a left on Hang Trong, and then right (west) to Nha Tho Street, behind the ANZ Bank. Consider a coffee break at **Highlands**, on the corner, see ⑪③.

St Joseph's Cathedral

Sitting at the west end of the street, **St Joseph's Cathedral** ❽ (Nha Tho Lon) is the one of the French Quarter's oldest buildings and Hanoi's only Gothic structure (closed noon–2pm for lunch). It was built by the French on the site of ancient Bao Thien Pagoda – demolished to make way for the cathedral – and consecrated on Christmas night in 1886. Many visitors have remarked that the Catholic cathedral resembles a smaller version of Paris's Notre-Dame. Inside are beautiful stained-glass windows and an altar decorated with gold leaf. Regular masses are usually packed, and at Christmas and Easter Vietnamese-style biblical scenes are mounted on the front facade.

Hanoi's Tube Houses

The Old Quarter still retains many 'tube houses', so called because of their narrow facades and long length. These single-storey shops belie their depth, containing dwellings at the rear and tiny courtyards. Feudal laws taxed shops according to their width – explaining why many are less than 3m (10ft) wide – and decreed buildings should be no higher than a passing royal palanquin, in deference to the emperor. Over the years, many buildings incorporated Western influences, like balconies and additional floors.

Opera House Area

Grab a taxi and head southeast to the intersection of Ly Thuong Kiet Street and Le Thanh Tong Street. As you head north, note the impressive 1920s building at the corner, which houses the medical annexe of the University of Hanoi, the former University of Indochina.

Le Thanh Tong and its surrounding streets are full of colonial villas housing diplomatic residences and embassies, but the most magnificent structure is the **Opera House** ❾, or Municipal Theatre (Nha Hat Lon), on the corner of Trang Tien Street. Built by the French (modelled on the neo-Baroque Paris Opera), it opened in 1911 to keep the colonials entertained (and remind them of home). Restored to its former grandeur and reopened in 1997, the Opera House is stunning, with a sweeping marble staircase, crystal chandeliers and red and gold leaf decor. Unfortunately, there are no tours or access, unless you have tickets for a cultural performance (details posted outside and at the ticket kiosk just inside). The Highlands Coffee at the Opera House is another good rest stop, as are the ice cream shops just across the way on Trang Tien Street. Adjacent to the Opera House is the luxury **Hilton Hanoi Opera Hotel**, with a pleasing facade that replicates the style of the Opera House. The interior, however, is very modern.

National Museum of Vietnamese History

Turn right into Trang Tien Street, walking five minutes towards the freeway, to visit the **National Museum of Vietnamese History** ❿ (Vien Bao Tang Lich Su Vietnam; tel: 04-3824 1384; daily 8am–4.30pm; charge). This stunning, renovated building, typifying hybrid Indochinese architecture, houses one of the city's best museums. It has easy-to-follow displays, surprisingly low propaganda content and excellent archaeological and historical relics. Displays include ancient Dong Son bronze drums,

Food and Drink

② CHA CA LA VONG

14 Cha Ca Street; tel: 04-3825 3929; daily B, L & D; $$$

One of Hanoi's most famous dishes, *cha ca* is the only thing served here – fish grilled on a clay brazier at your table – with rice noodles, peanuts and herbs. Overpriced given the no-frills surroundings and simple dishes – but the food is delicious.

③ HIGHLANDS COFFEE

6 Nha Tho Street; tel: 04-3936 3928; daily B, L & D; $$

Highlands is Vietnam's most popular upscale café chain. It is similar to a Western Starbucks-style café, with an excellent bakery, but the food is mostly Asian fusion, and all the coffee is grown in Vietnam. Service is top-notch. Seating is inside-only at this location.

Above from far left: St Jospeh's Cathedral; Hanoi's Opera House.

The scars of history

On 19 August 1945, the Viet Minh declared an independent democratic republic from the balcony of the Opera House, unfurling their banners in the process. Bullet holes from hand-to-hand fighting are still visible in the Hall of Mirrors inside.

Neolithic grave relics and clothes and artefacts belonging to the Nguyen emperors. Relics located in the grounds include the oldest epitaph in Southeast Asia, written in Sanskrit.

Afterwards, grab a taxi and head to the far southwest, formerly the French Quarter, for dinner at **Hoa Sua Training Restaurant**, see ④, on 28a Ha Hoi Street.

THE TEMPLE OF LITERATURE AND MUSEUMS

Around 8am the next morning, take a taxi to 59 Van Mieu Street for breakfast at **Koto**, across the street from the Temple of Literature, see ⑤.

Temple of Literature

The **Temple of Literature** ⓫ (Van Mieu; summer daily 7.30am–5pm, winter daily 8am–5pm; charge) was founded in 1070 as Vietnam's principal Confucian sanctuary and to honour Vietnamese scholars. In 1076 Vietnam's first university, the National Academy (Quoc Tu Giam), was established here to educate future mandarins in Confucian doctrine. Despite the capital moving to Hue in 1802, examinations continued until the early 20th century, before the French put a stop to them.

An oasis of calm and beauty, the ground plan is modelled on the birthplace of Confucius, with five interconnecting walled courtyards, complete with gateways and lotus ponds. In the third courtyard, 82 stone stelae, mounted on tortoises, are inscribed with the names of 1,307 laureates of state examinations held at the National Academy from 1442–1779. The fourth courtyard holds the main temple buildings – a red-lacquered **House of Ceremonies and Sanctuary**, dedicated to Confucius. The fifth, final courtyard once housed the National Academy buildings; unfortunately these were destroyed by French bombs in 1947 and replaced since with a new two-storey pavilion. Traditional music recitals are performed here, subject to demand (and a small contribution).

Vietnam Fine Arts Museum

The **Vietnam Fine Arts Museum** ⓬ (Bao Tang My Thuat), a five-minute walk away, is north of Van Mieu at 66 Nguyen Thai Hoc Street (tel: 04-3823 3084; daily 8am–5pm; charge). The museum holds around 14,000 artworks from the prehistoric to the present. Highlights include a multi-armed bodhisattva statue, 18th-century wooden Buddhist statues and some impressive folk art, including ancestral worship pictures on a handcrafted paper called *do*. Most of the displays concentrate on the development of Vietnamese art from the 20th century to the present through paintings and sculpture – silk and lacquer are given special emphasis.

Exploring Vietnamese ethnography
Hanoi's Museum of Ethnology was officially opened in 1997 by French President Jacques Chirac and designed with the help of the Musée de l'Homme in Paris. It is the finest of all of Vietnam's ethnic museums.

Vietnam Museum of Ethnology

Take a taxi to the far west side of town (about 20 minutes from the Fine Arts Museum) to the **Vietnam Museum of Ethnology** ⓭ (Bao Tang Dan Toc Hoc Vietnam, Nguyen Van Huyen Road; tel: 04-3756 2193; www.vme.org.vn; Tue–Sun 8.30am–5.30pm; charge) is perhaps Vietnam's most progressive museum. Before exploring the museum, grab a light lunch at **Baguette & Chocolat** behind the main building, see ⑥.

As a centre for research and conservation, the museum serves to promote a greater understanding of Vietnam's 54 ethnic minority groups. If you haven't the time to visit these ethnic groups, the museum is the next best thing to understand their diverse heritage, cultures and lifestyles. The museum has gathered nearly 15,000 ethnic artefacts from across Vietnam, including musical instruments, masks, baskets and garments, as well as maps, wall charts and photographs, which are superbly showcased. Dioramas depict scenes such as conical hat production, markets and various ritual ceremonies – illustrated by audiovisual tapes. There is even a reconstruction of a traditional Black Thai house. Check the boards outside the main entrance for information on daily water puppet shows. You will also find a permanent display of authentic, life-size minority dwellings, as well as a grave house behind the museum building.

After a long and leisurely visit through the extensive museum, take a taxi to the other side of West Lake (Ho Tay) and finish the evening at **Restaurant Bobby Chinn**, see ⑦, on 77 Xuan Dieu Street.

Above from far left: Temple of Literature; Fine Arts Museum; a Tibeto-Burmese costume and model Nha Rong houses, Ethnology Museum.

Food and Drink

④ HOA SUA TRAINING RESTAURANT

28A Ha Hoi Street; tel: 043-942 4448; daily B, L & D; $$$

Part of the Hoa Sua project for disadvantaged youth, housed in a beautiful restored villa. Service can be haphazard, but your patronage is for a good cause. The cuisine – French influenced with some Vietnamese – can be surprisingly good and great value.

⑤ KOTO

59 Van Mieu Street; tel: 04-3747 0337; www.koto.com.au; daily B, L & D; $$$

Koto serves tasty international food: the Mediterranean wraps and paninis, beer-battered fish and chips, lemongrass chicken skewers, spring rolls and buffet breakfast are all recommended. Koto is a non-profit project providing hospitality training for Hanoi's disadvantaged youth.

⑥ BAGUETTE & CHOCOLAT

Ethnology Museum; tel: 04-2243 1116; www.hoasuaschool.com; daily B & L; $$

This excellent bakery and café sits behind the main building at the Ethnology Museum. Seating is indoors and outside on the patio. The restaurant is run by Hoa Sua, a highly respected culinary school for disadvantaged youth. Try the citron tarts and pastries!

⑦ RESTAURANT BOBBY CHINN

77 Xuan Dieu Street, Tay Ho District; tel: 04-3719 2460; www.bobbychinn.com; daily B, L & D; $$$$

Restaurateur and chef Bobby Chinn is a global hybrid, and this is reflected in his pan-Pacific fusion cuisine. His fabulously opulent restaurant features a separate downstairs bar, silk drapes and excellent service. Smoking Egyptian shisha (water) pipes while you lie on scattered silk cushions is optional.

13

HANOI: HO CHI MINH'S LEGACY

A full-day tour which takes in the heart of Hanoi's political and diplomatic centre, including Ho Chi Minh's mausoleum, museum, stilt house and the One Pillar Pagoda. Explore the legacy left by the father of modern Vietnam.

DISTANCE 5.5km (3½ miles)
TIME A full day
START Ba Dinh Square
END Thanh Long Water Puppet Theatre
POINTS TO NOTE
This tour is for history buffs; it is unlikely to grab the interest of children. This tour can be combined with tour 12. Transportation is available within the city in the form of taxis and motorbikes.

While wandering the world, a young Vietnamese revolutionary, Nguyen Ai Quoc, better known as Ho Chi Minh, developed a strong sense of political consciousness. Ho founded the Indochinese Communist Party in Guangzhou, China, in 1930. After 30 years in self-imposed exile, Ho Chi Minh finally walked back across the border into Vietnam in 1941 and co-founded the League for the Independence of Vietnam (Viet Minh). His goal was not only independence from French colonial rule and Japanese occupation, but also 'the union of diverse nationalist groups under Communist direction'.

Ho formed the National Liberation Committee and called for an uprising, the August Revolution, after which the north and the rest of Vietnam came under Viet Minh control. On 2 September 1945, Ho established the Democratic Republic of Vietnam with his Declaration of Independence Speech in Ba Dinh Square, near where he would later lie in state. This date became Vietnam's National Day and was also to be the date of Ho's death.

After decades of war with the French and then the Americans, the 1973 Paris Accord provided a ceasefire and a withdrawal of US troops. However, Ho Chi Minh had already died in 1969 without seeing his vision of a unified Vietnam become a reality.

Regardless of one's own personal feelings about his legacy, there is no denying that Ho Chi Minh didn't merely have a strong influence, but is directly responsible for the reshaping and unification of modern Vietnam.

Here in Hanoi his legacy is most evident, with the the country's greatest monument, mausoleum and museum in his honour.

BA DINH SQUARE

Eat breakfast prior to departure and take a taxi to the Ho Chi Minh Mausoleum, passing the Vietnam Military History Museum, Cot Co Flag Tower (a remnant of the Citadel) and Highlands Café en route. Aim to be at your starting point – 8 Hung Vuong Street, near Chua Mot Cot Street, at Ba Dinh Square – by 8.30am.

The difference between the Old Quarter's fascinating chaos and **Ba Dinh Square** could not be more contrasting. Huge, austere Ba Dinh Square, with its Soviet-style architecture, is a sobering reminder of where you are – a socialist republic. This site of pilgrimage is where the former president of the Democratic Republic of Vietnam and founder of the Vietnamese Communist Party – Ho Chi Minh – lies for eternity in a massive, stark mausoleum (just like comrades Mao, Lenin and Stalin). In this very spot, Ho Chi Minh read out his Declaration of Independence on 2 September 1945: today, military parades and ceremonies occasionally take place here, watched by high-ranking party and government officials.

Walk along **Chua Mot Cot Street**, towards the intersection with **Dien Bien Phu Street**. French architectural influence is never far away; a prime example is the impressive **Ministry of Foreign Affairs** building. More fine examples of Alpine-style colonial buildings – housing embassies and diplomatic residences – are located at the top of Dien Bien Phu Street.

Colonial villas frame the square's northern boundary. Back at the square, on your left is the **National Assembly Hall** and beyond this, the **Heroes' Memorial**. You may catch the **Changing of the Guard** ceremony outside the mausoleum entrance, which usually takes place on the hour.

Above from far left: Mausoleum of Ho Chi Minh, patrolled by soldiers.

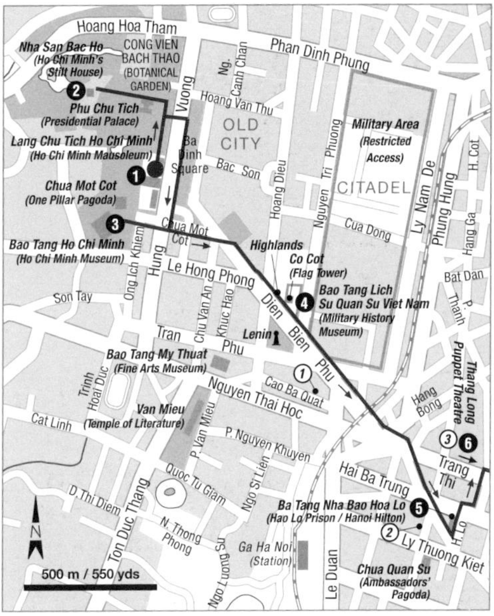

Mausoleum respect

The mausoleum has strict behavioural and dress codes as well as security measures. Dress respectfully for the Ho Chi Minh Mausoleum (absolutely do not wear shorts, T-shirts or short skirts) or you will be turned back.

HO CHI MINH MAUSOLEUM

The **Ho Chi Minh Mausoleum** ❶ (Lang Chu Tich Ho Chi Minh) was built by the Soviet Union as a gift to the Vietnamese (Apr–Oct Tue–Thur 7.30–10.30am, Sat–Sun 7.30–11am, Nov–Mar Tue–Thur 8–11am, Sat–Sun 8–11.30am; free). It was inaugurated on 29 August 1975 (although Ho Chi Minh died in 1969). At the arrival point, leave your bags and personal effects such as cameras and mobile phones at the designated cloakroom or at the 'collection points' nearby (hold on to your wallet/purse). Remember to collect your belongings before these close at 11am. Pass through security control and under the intimidating gaze of soldier guards; queue in strict line. As you enter the mausoleum, it's prudent to stop talking or laughing, take your hands out of your pockets (and take off your hat if you're wearing one) and adopt a respectful demeanour. If you forget, the guards will certainly remind you. Inside a cold room, you will slowly file past Ho Chi Minh's embalmed body lying in a glass casket.

Closed for 'Maintenance'

Ho Chi Minh's Mausoleum closes for 'maintenance' sometime during September to November. In the past, at this time, the body was packed off to Russia for re-embalming, much like Lenin's own corpse. Apparently this is now undertaken in Hanoi.

It's ironic that the egalitarian, unassuming Ho lies in a huge memorial; supposedly his last wish was to be cremated. However, given the reverence for the 'forefather of modern Vietnam', this wasn't considered a feasible option. Foreigners may find this whole process strange, but for most Vietnamese, paying respect to 'Uncle Ho' is a sacred task.

PRESIDENTIAL PALACE AND HO CHI MINH'S STILT HOUSE

Exit the other side, where you are ushered to the next part of the grounds, **Ho Chi Minh's Memorial Site** (summer 7.30–11am, 2–4pm, winter 8–11am, 1.30–4pm; charge) inside the Presidential Palace area.

The Presidential Palace

Walk through the wooded gardens, passing the magnificent **Presidential Palace**. Unless you have an invitation, this is the nearest you'll get to the restored colonial building, as it is closed to the public. Built in 1906, this was home to several governor-generals of Indochina and is now used by the president. For the last 15 years of his life, Ho used the Presidential Palace for government council and receiving guests, but because of his simple lifestyle, he refused to reside here.

Ho Chi Minh's Stilt House

Ho Chi Minh lived in two unassuming houses on the grounds instead. The first (along with a garage with his cars) is on your left (access isn't possible, but

peeks through the windows are), and the other, a specially constructed stilt house further to your right, beside a picturesque carp pond.

Ho Chi Minh's Stilt House ❷ (Nha San Bac Ho) was where Ho worked and lived from 1958–69. Beautifully preserved with varnished wood and split bamboo screens, the modestly furnished quarters consist of an upstairs study and bedroom, plus an open, ground-floor meeting room. It was in a rear building that Ho passed away on 2 September 1969.

HO CHI MINH MUSEUM AND ONE PILLAR PAGODA

Walk south on Hung Vuong Street, past the mausoleum to the Ho Chi Minh Museum compound, which also houses the One Pillar Pagoda.

The Ho Chi Minh Museum

The **Ho Chi Minh Museum** ❸ (Bao Tang Ho Chi Minh) is a massive angular, Soviet-style monstrosity (tel: 04-3846 3752; daily 8–11.30am, 2–4pm, except Mon, and Fri pm; charge). Dominating the tiny One Pillar Pagoda, the museum opened on 19 May 1990 (the 100th anniversary of Ho Chi Minh's birth). It celebrates Ho's revolutionary life, especially his exile years, and the pivotal role he played in Vietnam's history in the context of international communist development. As you walk through the unidirectional museum you will encounter exhibits of photos, documents and personal effects, such as his rubber sandals, walking stick and the disguise he used to flee Hong Kong. The exhibition departs from tradition with a surprisingly modern, almost surreal touch. Bizarre symbolic installations feature giant artificial fruit on enormous, lopsided furniture, a brick volcano and even a totem pole. Try figuring out the symbolism!

One Pillar Pagoda

The **One Pillar Pagoda** (Chua Mot Cot) is one of Hanoi's most recognised symbols. The original 11th-century version was blown up by French troops in 1954. This wooden pagoda, rising out of a lotus pond, is a newer, smaller version built in the late 1950s. The pagoda is meant to resemble a lotus blossom, a Buddhist symbol of purity. The pagoda's diminutive size (it's more of a small shrine, really), may strike some as comical, given its widely touted status as a national symbol.

MILITARY HISTORY MUSEUM AND FLAG TOWER

Cross to the east side of Ba Dinh Square then south on Dien Bien Phu Street, arriving at the nearby **Military History Museum** ❹ (Bao Tang Lich Su Quan Su Viet Nam; 28A Dien Bien Phu Street; tel: 04-3823 4264;

Above from far left: Presidential Palace; inside Ho Chi Minh Museum; One Pillar Pagoda.

The 'Hanoi Hilton'
Hanoi's notorious prison was dubbed the 'Hanoi Hilton' by US POWs incarcerated here during the war. These included Douglas Pete Peterson, the first US Ambassador to the Socialist Republic of Vietnam, and former presidential hopeful and US senator John McCain, who bailed out into Truc Bach Lake.

8–11.30am, 1–4.30pm, closed Mon and Fri; charge). The museum traces the development of Vietnam's armed forces through 30 galleries, from battles with the Mongols and Chinese, all the way up through America and the Khmer Rouge. Outside you'll see captured fighter planes, tanks and other military equipment. Prior to visiting the museum, either take lunch at the **Highlands Coffee** next door, or walk further down the road, crossing Tran Phu Street, then turning south (right on Le Duan Street), and west (left) into Cao Ba Quat for lunch a **Au Lac Do Brazil**, see 🍴①.

Beside the museum, the **Cot Co** (Flag Tower) is the only part of Emperor Gia Long's Citadel that is open to the public. Admission is free, so climb to the top for a fantastic view of the city.

HOA LO PRISON

Take a taxi or walk southeast on Dien Bien Phu Street, continuing down Tho Nhuom Street. Then take a left on Hoa Lo Street, arriving at **Hoa Lo Prison** ❺ (tel: 04-3824 6358; daily 8–11.30am, 1.30–4.30pm; charge). Opened in 1896, this walled prison compound once occupied an entire block. Known back then as Maison Centrale, it was the largest French prison in North Vietnam at the time. A small section now remains, preserved as a museum.

Below: performance at the Water Puppet Theatre.

Most of the museum concentrates on the plight of countless Vietnamese patriots and revolutionaries imprisoned and tortured here under French rule, pre-1954. Many grim, authentic relics remain, including instruments of torture, fetters, death-row cells and the guillotine – the way many inmates met their tragic deaths.

Towards the back, two fascinating rooms (if you can take the propaganda) document the capture, incarceration and subsequent release of American POWs through a collection of photographs, documents and attire.

DINNER AND WATER PUPPETS

Enjoy Hanoi's best pizza at **Classico**, see ⑪②, just around the corner on Quan Su Street, or catch a taxi north on Phu Doan Street, turning east (right) at Chau Cam, and eat at **La**, see ⑪③, at 25 Ly Quoc Su Street. After dinner, it's a 15-minute walk from La, northeast to the **Thang Long Water Puppet Theatre** ❻ (Nha Hat Mua Roi Thang Long; tel: 04-3825 5450; www.thanglongwaterpuppet.org) at 57 Dinh Tien Hoang Street on Hoan Kiem Lake. Water puppetry is one of the oldest indigenous forms of entertainment in Vietnam. Wooden puppets, which are manipulated by bamboo sticks hidden under water, play out stories based on fables as well as historical and daily events. The light-hearted performance is a good way to unwind after a day of ideology and war.

Food and Drink

① AU LAC DO BRAZIL
6A Cao Ba Quat; tel: 04-3845 5224; www.aulacdobrazil.com; daily L & D; $$$$
This all-you-can-eat Brazilian barbecque is a little unusual for Vietnam, though there are now three outlets in Hanoi and Ho Chi Minh City. Twelve types of meat are served for about $25 per person. The restaurant has a good wine list.

② CLASSICO CAFÉ & RESTAURANT
68 Quan Su Street; tel: 04-3941 2327; www.classico.com.vn; daily B, L & D; $$$
Classico serves up some of the best pizza in Hanoi, if not Vietnam: heavy, cheesy and loaded with toppings. Inside and outside garden seating is available. The private museum of ancient Dong Son relics inside the restaurant is delightful.

③ LA
25 Ly Quoc Su; tel: 04-3928 8933; daily B, L & D; $$$$
A dramatic entry with tall wooden double-doors opens to a casual bistro run by friendly and knowledgeable staff. The menu is a mix of Western tastes and Asian fusion. Food is a bit pricey but well designed and presented. The pork tenderloin is tasty, and the ample side dishes a delight.

Above from far left: Military History Museum; Hoa Lo Prison.

Plan ahead
Be sure to buy advanced tickets for the evening performance of the Thang Long Water Puppet Theatre first thing in the morning or the day before, as they tend to sell out, especially at weekends.

14

THE PERFUME PAGODA

A day trip to the ethereal homeland of Buddhism in Vietnam, the Perfume Pagoda, is one of the highlights of Hanoi. The boat ride alone is worth the trip, but the hike to the 'most beautiful temple under the southern sky' is the grand finale.

DISTANCE A 120km (74-mile) return drive southwest of Hanoi, followed by a 3-hour return boat ride, and finally a 4km (2½-mile) return hike.
TIME A full day
START/END Yen Vi Village Boat Pier on the Yen River
POINTS TO NOTE
Don't make this trip during weekends and festivals, in order to avoid crowds. Identical organised tours, sold by every hotel and ticket office in Hanoi, are the easiest way to reach the Perfume Pagoda (prices range from $20–30), though this eliminates the option of visiting other temples or grottoes in the area. The tour requires considerable walking up steep inclines. Children and the elderly especially may wish to use the optional gondola instead.

Package deals
Most Hanoi tour operators run this tour with lunch, entrance fees, transport and guide included in the price; other attractions are sometimes visited en route.

The site of the oddly misnamed **Perfume Pagoda** (Chua Huong; daily 7.30am–6pm; charge) comprises a group of temples covering an area of 30 sq km (11½ sq miles). Built into the limestone cliffs of the 'Ancient Vestiges of Perfume Grotto' (Dong Huong Tich), otherwise known as the Perfume Mountains, the earliest temples date from the 15th century. By the early 20th century there were over 100. This area was the site for some bitter uprisings against the French colonialists and as a result, several temples were destroyed during the late 1940s. Fortunately, the area retains much of its natural splendour and is regarded as one of the most beautiful spots in Vietnam.

THE BOAT RIDE

The journey by road south from Hanoi brings you to riverside **Yen Vi village** ❶, where you board a shallow metal-bottomed boat (there are no roads to the Perfume Pagoda). For many, the 90-minute boat trip along the wide, swiftly flowing **Yen River** is almost as worthwhile as visiting the pagoda itself. Here fishermen wade the crystal waters among floating graves of their ancestors. As the oarsman steers the boat along the river, relax and take in the mesmerising landscape of jagged limestone hills.

Above: boat ride on the Yen River to the Perfume Pagoda.

THE MOUNTAIN HIKE

Disembark from the boat at the base of the Huong Tich Mountains for your 1½–2-hour hike. **Thien Tru Temple** ❷ or Heavenly Kitchen (a reference to a Vietnamese constellation, not the secular noodle stalls that cluster around it) reaches up the mountain ahead. Most groups will have lunch at the **food stalls**, see 🍴①, here. From here, weary travellers can take the convenient **cable car** ❸ (*cap treo*; charge) or continue up the path to the right of the temple, which leads to the destination 2km (1¼ miles) away. On your return, you may wish to climb the stone staircase to the right of the path leading to the **Tien Son Temple** ❹, where there are unusual stone musical instruments made from stalagmites.

After 10 minutes along the main path, you will see a shrine built over a spring. Legend has it that if you bathe in **Giai Oan** ❺, your spirit will be purified and false charges against you cleared. Where the path thins and becomes a little steeper, you will see the shrine for the **'Goddess of the Mountains'** ❻ (Cua Vong). Your destination lies just below the summit of this mountain.

HUONG TICH GROTTO

You will see the portal and 120 stone steps bedecked with Buddhist flags leading down to the smoky depths of **Huong Tich Grotto** ❼. Chinese characters etched on the outside of the cave in 1770 declare this to be the 'most beautiful grotto under the southern sky'. Romantically inclined Vietnamese compare the cave to a dragon's mouth, with the steps leading into the cavern as its throat.

The huge stalagmites at the mouth of the cave bear curious names. The bulbous one in the centre is called

Food and Drink

① FOOD STALLS
Located at the boat pier; daily B, L & D; $$
There are a dozen humble food stalls located at the boat landing on the base of Huong Tich Mountain. Usually a group lunch at a stall of the guide's choosing is part of package tours. Food is local fare (mostly stir-fried vegetables and fried fish) with rice. Drinks cost extra.

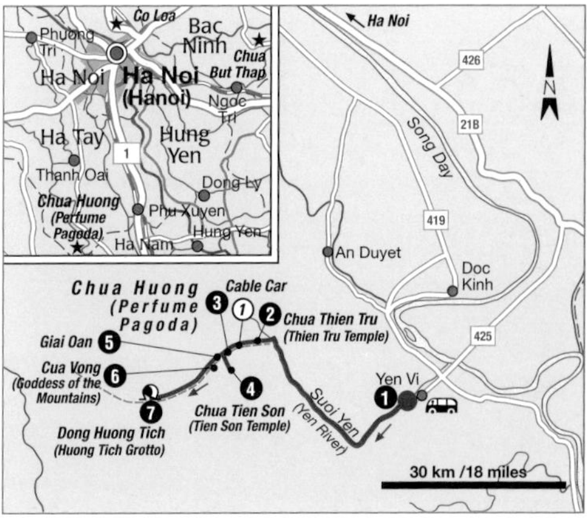

Top and above: in Huong Tich Grotto.

the **Rice Stack**, while other stalagmites inside have been named the **Mountain of the Teenage Goddess**, **Silkworms Chamber**, **Cocoons Rack** and the **Heap of Coins**. The bell near the entrance dates from 1655 and is only beaten on ceremonial occasions.

ALTARS, INCENSE AND STATUES

As your eyes grow accustomed to the darkness you will see many altars and statues of deities twinkling with candlelight. The central one houses an important statue of **Quan Am** (Goddess of Mercy), the female personification of the Buddha. Her androgynous figure is swathed in a diaphanous fabric. According to folklore, the bodhisattva Avalokiteshvara transformed himself into the female deity Quan Am here, and the shrine is dedicated to her. Through the haze of incense smoke you will see women with offerings of fruit and incense. Many barren women come to pray for children from the goddess inside.

For many Vietnamese this is the most important religious area in the whole of Vietnam, and many devout Buddhists will try to visit the shrine at least once in their lives. It is said that the Buddha himself may have visited this area once, leaving his 'perfumed footprint', the first of many theories about the origins of the name 'Perfume'.

Today, monks still conduct services on request. If you come across one, listen for the soothing pitter-patter of Buddhist drums keeping time with the sound of condensation droplets falling in the cave.

For your return journey, choose a nice spot on the boat to enjoy the full scenery that has inspired generations of Vietnamese poets and monks.

Walking Conditions

During the first two months after Tet (roughly February/March or March/April depending on the lunar calendar), the Perfume Pagoda can get very crowded with pilgrims, making for a frustrating (or alternatively, highly interesting) experience. The walk up the mountain is steep and can be quite tough going, so wear sensible shoes and bring a bottle of water. In the summer, it can get very hot and sweaty. Boats have no cover, so wear sun protection. As there are no places to eat along the way, bring a picnic lunch if your tour package does not include one, plus a torch for the caves.

SA PA

15

A former French hill station near the Chinese border, Sa Pa offers breathtaking mountain scenery, trekking and close encounters with ethnic minorities. Spend a couple of days visiting nearby villages and soaking up the highland ambience.

The French had the right idea when they made Sa Pa their hill station in the first half of the 20th century. Sa Pa's cool climate at 1,600m (5,249ft) is similar to that of the Alps, a welcome refuge from the stifling humidity and a reminder of home. Located 360km (223 miles) northwest of Hanoi and dramatically perched on the edge of a high plateau, Sa Pa has a stunning location, framed by soaring blue peaks and sweeping valleys dotted with paddy fields and ethnic-minority villages.

Since the French departed, Sa Pa was forgotten for about half a century until foreigners rediscovered it in the 1990s. Currently undergoing major tourism development with a number of new hotels under construction, the town may have lost a little of its soul, but it is still charming. It is the perfect base to explore the stupendous outlying scenery and ethnic minority villages, where traditional daily life carries on as it has for centuries. And relaxing on a balcony – with Mount Fansinpan (Phan Si Pan) almost within touching distance – it doesn't get much better than this.

The best time to visit is September to November and March to May. The

DISTANCE Day 1: 2km (1¼ miles) walking; Day 2: 4km (2½ miles) walking, 23km (14 miles) driving
TIME 2 days
START Day 1: Catholic chapel; Day 2: Cat Cat village
END Day 1: radio tower; Day 2: Ta Phin village
POINTS TO NOTE
Make sure you book your return train ticket and hotel in advance. Trains can be very full, especially at weekends. Night trains depart daily from Tran Quy Cap station (behind the main station on Le Duan Street) at 10pm, arriving at Lao Cai station the following morning at 6–7am (four-berth, soft sleeper with fan or air conditioning costs around US$19 one way; for more comfort, book Tulico berths, 5 Hang Can Street; tel: 043-828 7806; www.tulico-Sa Pa.com.vn). If money is no object, book a package with the Victoria Sa Pa Resort, which transfers guests on board its luxurious Victoria Express Train *(see p.115)*.

Above: Sa Pa's Catholic chapel *(see p.92)*.

Vendor management
Hmong and Dzao ladies are exceedingly friendly and polite, but very persistent. Unlike other parts of Vietnam, the local vendors will follow you all morning – everywhere you go – until you've made a purchase. Don't bother appeasing them right away; they will just be replaced by others. The best strategy is simply to smile, be patient, and make the most of the extra company.

rainy summer months, particularly July and August, are Sa Pa's busiest months (with the most expensive hotel rates), when Hanoians flock here to escape the heat. Temperatures can plummet in winter, with frost and occasional snow.

After a nine-hour train ride from Hanoi, catch a minivan up the mountain to Sa Pa. Local hotels can organise transfers from Lao Cai, but there are also tourist minibuses (a ticket costs about 30,000 dong) which await incoming trains for the 39km (24-mile) drive to Sa Pa. As you zigzag your way uphill from Lao Cai, enjoying spectacular views of the breathtaking Hoang Lien Son mountain range, bear in mind that the French colonialists were carried up here by sedan chair.

Food and Drink

① HIGHLAND BAKERY HOTEL RESTAURANT

50 Cau May Street; tel: 020-387 1870; daily B, L & D; $$$

Highland is an excellent bakery and wifi café with great coffee. Sandwiches and Western favourites are the main feature. Comfortable, seating is available in the wood-furnished interior. A sister bakery is also located at Fansipan mountain.

② THE GECKO RESTURANT

Ham Rom Street, near the Post Office; tel: 020-387 1504; daily B, L & D; $$$

The Gecko Restaurant is Sa Pa's first French restaurant and one of the original expat venues. Italian and American favourites also feature on the menu: pizza, hamburgers, pancakes, spaghetti and more. There is also a sister 'Le Petit Gecko' on Xuan Vien Street.

③ VIET EMOTION RESTAURANT AND TAPAS BAR

27 Cau May Street; tel: 020-387 2559; www.vietemotion.com; daily B, L & D; $$$$

This cosy restaurant bills itself as a tapas bar, but the menu items are mostly popular Vietnamese fare, hotpots and backpacker favourites like burgers, sandwiches and pasta. It's pricey but popular, with seating indoors and out.

Above: brocade embroidery by a woman in Sa Pa; the costume of a Red Dao woman.

AROUND TOWN

After checking into your hotel in the morning, get a late breakfast at **Highland Bakery Hotel Restaurant**, see ① on 50 Cau May Street. You may also want to get a picnic lunch.

Sa Pa Market

Afterwards, walk up the road to the square with the quaint little **Catholic chapel ❶** (Nha Tho Sa Pa) and explore the **town market ❷** from there. You'll encounter lots of Dzao and H'mong ladies selling blankets, silver trinkets, jaw harps and other handicrafts and souvenirs. Keep an eye out for another unique item in the butcher stalls: dog meat.

In the recent past, Sa Pa used to be sold on the pretext of a Saturday night 'Love Market', where young minori-

ties coyly met potential suitors in the town centre. This form of voyeuristic tourism, however, has been frowned on, and the tradition has moved to a more secluded area.

Walks

In the afternoon consider a hike around the lake and park, northeast of the town square, for scenic views of the modern town. As you pass to the lake you'll pass **The Gecko Restaurant** on Ham Rom Street, which makes a good lunch stop, see ②. Afterwards, hike up to the **radio tower** ❸, about 300m/yds behind the chapel, for spectacular views of the town and valley below.

Nightlife

Late in the afternoon walk south on Cau May Street to the tourist area, where you'll encounter an array of welcoming Alpine shops, restaurants and bars. Grab dinner at **Viet Emotion Restaurant and Tapas Bar** on 27 Cau May Street, see ③.

H'MONG AND DAO VILLAGES

The main reason to come to Sa Pa is the opportunity to trek through ethnic minority villages and enjoy overnight homestays and hospitality in local stilt houses, especially since government restrictions have been lifted. Several outlying villages – Cat Cat, Ta Van, Sin Chai, Lao Chai and Ta Phin – make pleasant and relatively easy treks.

Above from far left: in front of the Catholic chapel; Red Dao women in Ta Phin village; rice terraces.

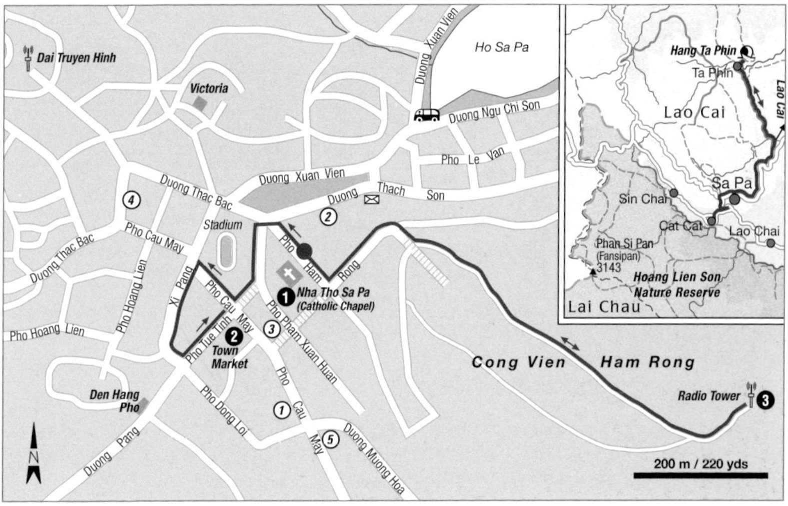

Start the morning of your second day with breakfast at **Baguette & Chocolat** on Thac Bac Street, northwest of the town square, see ⑭④. Ask the bakery to pack a lunch for you, or else pick something up in the Sa Pa market as you walk 3km (2 miles) southwest of town down Phan Si Street to **Cat Cat village**. Cat Cat is a beautiful, traditional Black H'mong village perched on the slopes of a hanging valley. Walk down the steep paths through the village to the river below, and then catch a motorbike back to Sa Pa.

For the afternoon, arrange a motorbike or guided tour *(see right)* to **Ta Phin village**, 10km (6 miles) from Sa Pa back towards Lao Cai, with a marked turnoff. Get dropped off at the start of this traditional Red Dao village, then walk through to the other side and visit the caves on the hill. Children will be eager to guide you into the caves with a flashlight for a tip.

Return to Sa Pa for a romantic dinner at **Sa Pa Lotus Restaurant** at 34 Cau May Street in the backpacker area, see ⑭⑤.

OUTLYING ETHNIC-MINORITY VILLAGES AND MARKETS

As villages close to Sa Pa are becoming increasingly commercialised, many operators are now venturing further afield, hiking to more remote mountain villages and scenery. Try to trek with a local guide, as they understand the local dialects, etiquette and customs better and are able to explain a good

Ethnic Minorities

Nearly two-thirds of Vietnam's ethnic-minority groups live in the northern mountainous regions – hence the name *Les montagnards*. Each with their own distinctive dress, customs and dialects, they subsist mostly through farming – rice and maize – cultivated on terraced fields. Sa Pa's main groups are the Giay, Tay, Xa Pho, but predominantly the Black H'mong and Red Dao. The Black H'mong are totally at ease with foreigners, and are recognisable by their indigo-blue hemp attire. Many H'mong females are excellent local guides, speak good English and have savvy sales techniques. On the streets of Sa Pa, they literally mob tourists with their handicraft wares. The Red Dao (pronounced 'Zao') are generally shyer but more striking with their scarlet turban-style headdress, embroidered clothes and often shaved head and eyebrows.

Above from far left: Black H'mong people; silver jewellery for sale in Sa Pa; Mount Fansipan viewed from Sa Pa.

deal more. Bring good walking boots, repellent, water and medical kit.

A number of fascinating but remote weekly ethnic-minority markets – located several hours from Sa Pa – offer a glimpse into much more traditional market life. Can Cau (Saturday), Coc Ly (Tuesday) and Muong Hom (Sunday), all found near the Chinese border, are highly recommended. Colourful, vibrant Bac Ha Market starts early Sunday morning in Bac Ha, roughly 80km (50 miles) east of Sa Pa.

Recommended local tour operators are: Handspan Adventure Travel (8 Cau May Street; tel: 020-387 2110; www.handspan.com); Topas Adventure Vietnam (24 Muong Hoa Street; tel: 020-387 1331; www.topastravel.vn); and Tulico (Darling Hotel, Thac Bac Street; tel: 020-387 1349; www.tulico-Sa Pa.com.vn).

MOUNT FANSIPAN

Looming ominously over Sa Pa, **Mount Fansipan** (Phan Si Pan) entices the more adventurous to conquer its summit, conditions permitting. The mountain stands at 3,143m (10,311ft) in the middle of Hoang Lien Son Nature Reserve, 5km (3 miles) from Sa Pa. Vietnam's highest mountain offers stunning panoramic views.

While it is not too technically demanding, climbing Fansipan is still a challenging experience. It can take several days up steep, overgrown trails. The time required is very much dependent on weather conditions. If you decide to make the ascent up Mount Fansipan, make sure that you arrange the trip with experienced operators that offer two- to four-day packages with all the necessary porters, guides and equipment, like tents and cooking facilities. Topas Eco-lodge (tel: 020-387 2404; www.topas-eco-lodge.com) is highly recommended for accommodation, and has 25 individual, eco-managed and solar-powered lodges set atop two remote hills, about a 1½-hour drive from Sa Pa.

Food and Drink

④ BAGUETTE & CHOCOLAT

Thac Bac Street; www.hoasuaschool.com; tel: 020-387 1766; daily B, L & D; $$$

Baguette & Chocolat has a big fireplace and cosy atmosphere which is a welcome comfort in the cold evenings. This bakery, café and restaurant is part of the Hoa Sua training programme for disadvantaged youth, with branches in Hanoi *(see p.81)*. The menu includes lots of delightful pastries, tarts and tasty sandwiches.

⑤ SA PA LOTUS

34 Cau May Street; tel: 020-387 3567; daily B, L & D; $$$

Sa Pa Lotus is another cosy, candlelit venue with a romantic setting. The restaurant offers both Vietnamese and Western favourites. Try the imported Australian beef and lamb or the excellent breakfast buffet spread.

Stay warm

Sa Pa and the Northern Highlands is the coldest region in Vietnam. Especially when visiting in winter month, be sure to pack some warm clothing. Be aware that many budget hotels and restaurants do not have heating and it gets quite chilly at night.

16

HALONG BAY

Spend two or three days cruising around Halong Bay, one of the most magnificent natural splendours of Asia. Swathed in legends and beauty and only about three hours from Hanoi, this World Heritage Site should not be missed.

DISTANCE Dependent on tour operator and length of tour
TIME 2 or 3 days
START/END Hanoi
POINTS TO NOTE
Explore Halong Bay by boat. It pays to go on an organised tour. Generally, these offer a package of meals, guide, boat, accommodation and transfers. Boats depart daily from Bai Chay Tourist Wharf in Ha Long City, 165km (102 miles) east of Hanoi by road.

Few could fail to be impressed with Halong Bay, with over 3,000 limestone islands jutting out of emerald-green waters in the Gulf of Bac Bo. In an area covering 1,500 sq km (579 sq miles), sampans, junks, fishing boats – and many tourist boats – sail past a fairy-tale backdrop of mostly uninhabited limestone karsts, which yield grottoes, secluded coves, coral beaches and hidden lagoons. No wonder it became a Unesco World Heritage Site in 1994.

The best time to visit **Halong Bay** (Vinh Ha Long) is in warmer weather from April to October, as you can

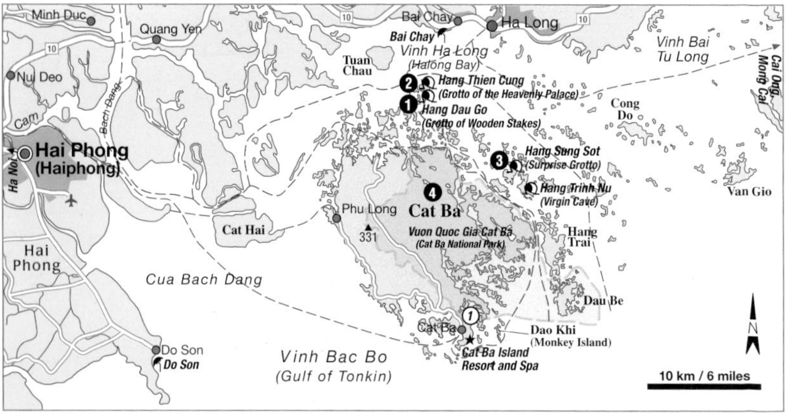

Food and Drink

① THE GREEN MANGO

Group 19, Block 4, Cat Ba Island; tel: 031 388-7151; www.greenmango.vn; daily B, L & D; $$$$

One of the finest restaurants in the bay. The restaurant has a tastefully decorated, seaside atmosphere and serves Western, Vietnamese and fusion cuisines. Seafood barbecue is the speciality. Other great items include fish and chips and creative desserts.

swim off the boat and relax on sundecks. However, during the typhoon season, which peaks in August, boats may cancel trips due to bad weather.

Halong Bay looks the stuff of legends – and it is. Ha Long means 'Descending Dragon', originating from the myth that a celestial dragon once flung itself headlong into the sea, its swishing tail digging deep valleys and crevices in the earth. As it descended into the sea, these filled with water, creating the bay.

The tour begins with a three- to four-hour road journey from Hanoi to Ha Long City, where you will board the boat contracted by your tour provider.

ISLANDS AND GROTTOES

Legends aside, geologists believe that the karst outcrops were formed by a giant limestone seabed eroding until only pinnacles remained behind. Your boat will visit a couple of the 15 caves open to the public, while en route. Tickets are purchased at the Tourist Wharf or are included in tour packages. The best known is found on the island nearest to Ha Long City: the **Grotto of Wooden Stakes** ❶ (Hang Dau Go), where General Tran Hung Dao amassed hundreds of stakes prior to his 1288 victory. On the same island, the **Grotto of the Heavenly Palace** ❷ (Hang Thien Cung) has some impressive stalactites and stalagmites, as does **Surprise Grotto** ❸ (Hang Sung Sot) on an island further south.

CAT BA ISLAND

After a night on the boat, where you will also eat your meals, spend the following morning enjoying activities on the water. In the afternoon, visit **Cat Ba Island** ❹, the largest in Halong Bay at 354 sq km (136 sq miles), which offers a spectacular, rugged landscape of forested limestone peaks, coral reefs, coastal mangrove and freshwater swamps, lakes and waterfalls. Almost three quarters of the island and its adjacent waters form a national park with diverse flora and fauna. Some boats dock in the fishing harbour, where mini-hotels and basic tourist services are located. Spend a night here if possible and hike to see the endemic Cat Ba langurs (monkeys). Eat dinner at **The Green Mango** along the shore, see ①, and then head back to Hanoi the following morning.

Above from far left: exploring fishing villages by rowboat in Halong Bay; Cat Co Beach on Cat Ba Island.

Tour Operators

All tour operators use engine-powered wooden boats, most with private cabins. **Buffalo Tours** (tel: 04-3828 0702; www.buffalotours.com) operates two luxury junks (five to eight cabins) with kayaking options; two- to three-day cruises start from US$159. **Handspan Adventure Travel** (tel: 04-3926 2828; www.handspan.com) offers two- to three-day options on their Aloha junks from US$115, and on the high-end Lagoon Explorer junks with four cabins from US$167. **Exotissimo** (tel: 04-3828 2150; www.exotissimo.com) has a good range of cruising and kayaking options at comparable rates.

CAO

CƠ SỞ SẢN XUẤT NƯỚC MẮM NHỈ CÁ CƠM
THANH THẾ
Nước mắm nhỉ cá cơm
LOẠI 1

DIRECTORY

A user-friendly alphabetical listing of practical information, plus hand-picked hotels and restaurants, clearly organised by area, to suit all budgets and tastes. Select nightlife listings are also included here.

A

AGE RESTRICTIONS

The age of consent in Vietnam is 18. There is not a legal drinking age minimum in Vietnam. Driving age is 15 (a Vietnamese licence is required, even for foreign visitors).

C

CHILDREN

Children are universally adored in Vietnam, so youngsters will be welcome almost anywhere. Most of the big cities have a water park and/or a zoo of some sort. Plus there are good beaches along the entire coast and excellent national parks to explore. Leave the buggy at home as footpaths are generally not pedestrian-friendly; a chest-mounted baby carrier is more practical. Infants and small children usually have free admission at venues.

CLOTHING

Bring casual, lightweight clothing in natural fabrics, which offer the most comfort in the humidity and heat. If you plan to spend time in the Highlands, then a light jacket or fleece and long trousers – especially in winter – are advisable. Rain gear, including a small umbrella, is a good idea, as it's always raining somewhere in Vietnam.Sandals or footwear that can be easily slipped off are best; shoes should be removed before entering homes and some shops.

CRIME AND SAFETY

In general, Vietnam is a safe country to travel in and violent crimes against foreigners are rare. Petty theft and robbery, however, are very common. In big cities, especially Ho Chi Minh City, tourists are often the victims of pickpockets, sometimes in the form of children and women with babies, or snatch-and-grab thieves. It's not uncommon to have phones, laptops and even sunglasses snatched by passing motorcyclists. Always leave valuables in a hotel safe; when you must carry cash, put it in a money belt worn inside your clothes. When walking or travelling in a cyclo, keep a hand firmly on bags and cameras, and on buses or trains always stay with your luggage. If you travel by train, bring a cable lock to secure your bags to your bed frame when you are sleeping.

CUSTOMS

Visitors to Vietnam are required to fill in a detailed customs declaration upon arrival. Customs may inspect your luggage to verify that you have made a correct declaration. Currency in excess of US$7,000, and multiple electronics which look like they might be imported for resell, should be declared. Your items may be inspected to check for anything

considered culturally or politically sensitive (including religious items), but this is usually only a concern for mailed parcels. Visitors must keep a copy of the customs declaration form to show customs officials upon leaving Vietnam.

D

DISABLED TRAVELLERS

With all the traffic, scarcity of lifts and the sheer amount of people out and about on the streets, disabled travellers do not have an easy time in Vietnam. The roads are extremely treacherous and drivers don't tend to stop, even for the disabled, especially in the major cities. It's a contentious issue that a country with so many disabled citizens hasn't done more to accommodate them. Thankfully, it's not impossible for adventurous disabled people with an easygoing attitude to get by. Generally the bigger hotels have wheelchair access, special toilets and lifts.

E

ELECTRICITY

The voltage in the cities and towns is generally 220V, 50 cycles. Electric sockets are standard European and/or American, but bring an adaptor just in case. If you bring a computer to Vietnam, you should consider using a surge suppressor to protect its circuit.

EMBASSIES AND CONSULATES

Embassies in Hanoi

Australia: 8 Dao Tan St, Ba Dinh District; tel: 04-3831 7755; www.vietnam.embassy.gov.au.

Canada: 31 Hung Vuong Street; tel: 04-3734 5000; www.dfait-maeci.gc.ca/vietnam.

New Zealand: 63 Ly Thai To Street; tel: 04-3824 1481; www.nzembassy.com.

UK: 31 Hai Ba Trung Street; tel: 04-3936 0500; www.uk-vietnam.org.

US: 7 Lang Ha Street; tel: 04-3831 4590; http://vietnam.usembassy.gov.

Consulates in Ho Chi Minh City

Australia: 5B Ton Duc Thang Street, District 1; tel: 08-3829 6035; www.hcmc.vietnam.embassy.gov.au.

Canada: 235 Dong Khoi Street, District 1; tel: 08-3827 9899.

New Zealand: 235 Dong Khoi Street, District 1; tel: 08-3822 6907.

UK: 25 Le Duan Street, District 1; tel: 08-3829 8433; bcghcmc@hcm.vnn.vn.

US: 4 Le Duan Street, District 1; tel: 08-3822 9433; http://hochiminh.usconsulate.gov.

EMERGENCIES

The unpleasant truth is that foreigners are on their own for emergencies. There are no hotlines, police are generally unhelpful, and hospitals have been known to refuse treatment of foreigners with serious injuries without proof of

Above from far left: celebrating Tet, the Vietnamese Lunar New Year; in Tan Son Nhat Airport, Ho Chi Minh City.

Budgeting

While still inexpensive for most Western travellers, Vietnam is not as cheap as it was just a few years ago. A local beer costs less than $1, while a whole bottle of Da Lat wine is just under $2. A meal at a street vendor costs about $1, while main courses at a moderate tourist restaurant would be $5, and at a reasonably expensive restaurant $10 or $15. Basic guest-house rooms run at $10–15, rooms at moderate hotels $25–35, and resorts from $80 to several hundred. A taxi ride from the airport to downtown HCMC will average $5, while the same ride in Hanoi is $10. Bus tickets between major cities average $5–6.

Green issues
Environmental issues are not taken seriously in Vietnam. Pollution, deforestation, poaching of wildlife and sanitation are all very serious and ongoing problems. Visitors can do their part by not eating exotic animals (including those claimed to be captive-raised, which usually are not) or buying products made from wild animals. Air travel produces a huge amount of carbon dioxide and is a significant contributor to global warming. If you would like to offset your flight, a number of organisations can do this for you, using online 'carbon calculators', which tell you how much you need to donate. In the UK travellers can visit www.climatecare.org or www.carbonneutral.com; in the US log on to www.climatefriendly.com or www.sustainabletravelinternational.org.

the ability to pay. The best thing to do is request assistance from one's hotel or tour company. Always buy travel insurance and head to Bangkok for serious medical emergencies.

ETIQUETTE

Most meals are eaten 'family style' with shared courses. It is considered polite for hosts occasionally to dish out the best morsels into the guests' bowl throughout the meal. In many dining establishments it is common to discard table scraps on the floor or on the table itself. Observe what others do, and do likewise. Never leave chopsticks sticking upright in your bowl as it symbolises an offering to the dead.

Anyone visiting the inner sanctum of a Buddhist temple will be required to remove their shoes and hat. Temples administered by the government as 'cultural relics' (tourist attractions) generally require men to wear a shirt and trousers, and women to wear a modest top with skirt or trousers. However, such dress is not required to visit most pagodas, and Vietnamese men and women will often show up in shorts and T-shirts.

G

GAY AND LESBIAN ISSUES

Travel in Vietnam is a relative breeze for gay people. In the last few years, HCMC's gay scene has come out in force. It's common to see very open Vietnamese couples at clubs and cafés downtown. Same-sex couples will not be questioned about sharing a hotel room, but if guests stay for an extended period, there will be presumptions made.

It is quite common to see open affection between the same sexes in cafés or on the street among the Vietnamese. Men can often be seen holding hands, and women too, although this is usually just a sign of deep friendship. On the other hand, it is quite rare to see open affection between men and women.

H

HEALTH

Inoculations

Immunisation against hepatitis (A and B), Japanese encephalitis and tetanus are strongly encouraged. Malaria and dengue fever are prevalent throughout Vietnam, but malaria is rarely see in tourist areas. Dengue, on the other hand, is very common in both rural and urban areas. The best protection is prevention. Sleep under a mosquito net at night, use potent DEET repellent on exposed skin at all times, and where possible try to wear long-sleeved tops and trousers. Malaria-carrying mosquitoes are most active during the night, but the mosquitoes that spread dengue are most active during the day.

If you are travelling in remote areas, consult with a knowledgeable doctor to

determine what anti-malarial drugs are best suited for your travels. For more information, check the website of the Centre for Disease Control (CDC) in Atlanta, United States: www.cdc.gov.

Healthcare and Insurance

Healthcare in Vietnam is pay-as-you-go. Foreigners are advised to have travel insurance covering emergency evacuations.

Pharmacies and Hospitals

All hospitals have 24-hour pharmacies. Private pharmacies, open late, are also common in cities.

Hanoi

Hanoi French Hospital, 1 Phuong Mai Street, Dong Da District; tel: 04-3577 1100.
Vietnam-Korea Friendship Clinic, 12 Chu Van An Street, Ba Dinh District; tel: 04-3843 7231.

Ho Chi Minh City

Columbia Saigon, 8 Alexandre de Rhodes Street; tel: 08-3829 8520.
HCMC Family Medical Practice, Diamond Plaza, 34 Le Duan Street; tel: 08-3822 7848.

L

LANGUAGE

English is now spoken in most hotels, restaurants and shops catering to tourists but learning a little of the language goes a long way.

Numbers

0 *khong*
1 *mot*
2 *hai*
3 *ba*
4 *bon*
5 *nam*
6 *sau*
7 *bay*
8 *tam*
9 *chin*
10 *muoi*

Days of the Week

Monday *thu hai*
Tuesday *thu ba*
Wednesday *thu tu*
Thursday *thu nam*
Friday *thu sau*
Saturday *thu bay*
Sunday *chu nhat*

Basics

Yesterday *hom qua*
Today *hom nay*
Tomorrow *ngay mai*
Yes *vang* (north), *da* (south)
No *khong*
Hello *xin chao*
Goodbye *tam biet*
My name is... *ten toi la...*
How are you? *Ban co khoe khong?*
Thank you *cam on*
Thank you very much *cam on rat nhieu*

Above: football on the beach.

Internet

Internet cafés with computer terminals have lost popularity with the rapid proliferation of free wifi, and the fact that most hotels have one or two computers with free access to the internet for their guests. Most of the old internet cafés now run online games instead of providing general internet use. Most cafés, hotels and restaurants (the last catering more to foreigners) have free wifi.

Left luggage
Tan Son Nhat Airport (tel: 08-3844 6665), which services Ho Chi Minh City, has left-luggage facilities (daily 7.30am–11pm) at both terminals. All hotels and guesthouses offer a left-luggage service; usually it is free, but some may levy a small daily fee for extended periods.

Lost property
Unfortunately there is very little that can be done to recover lost or stolen property in Vietnam. In the event, ask someone at your hotel to help you file a police report for insurance purposes, though police may not always be cooperative.

Sorry/Excuse me *xin loi*
Can you help me? *Ban co the giup toi duoc khong?*
No problem/you're welcome *khong co gi*
Do you speak English? *Ban co noi duoc tieng Anh khong?*
I don't understand *Toi khong hieu*

M

MEDIA

All Vietnamese media, whether print, broadcast, recordings or performances, must undergo a lengthy government censorship and approval process before they go public.

Foreign newspapers and magazines can be purchased in larger bookstores in downtown HCMC and Hanoi, as well as some upscale hotels (although they aren't always current). Street vendors in tourist areas often sell second-hand copies too.

Newspapers

Vietnam has several English-language government-run newspapers, including *Viet Nam News* (http://vietnamnews.vnagency.com.vn), *Vietnam Investment Review* (www.vir.com.vn), with its helpful weekly supplement called *Timeout* (www.vir.com.vn/client/timeout), *Vietnam Economic Times* (www.vneconomy.vn), with its weekly supplement *The Guide*, and *Viet Nam Net* (www.english.vietnamnet.vn).

Magazines

The Word is the most popular English-language lifestyle and travel magazine, aimed at an expat audience, with separate editions in HCMC (www.wordhcmc.com) and Hanoi.

Radio

Two stations transmit English-language programmes on a variety of subjects several times a day on FM radio.

Television

Most hotels, restaurants, bars and cafés now have cable or satellite television with access to CNN, BBC, Australia Network, Star TV, Discovery, HBO, Cartoon Network, MTV Asia and more. The quality of transmission is generally poor in rural areas; it's not uncommon to be interrupted in middle of a programme with a sudden switch to another channel.

MONEY

Vietnam's unit of currency, the dong (pronounced 'dome', and abbreviated as VND), currently circulates in banknotes of 500,000, 100,000, 50,000, 20,000, 10,000, 5,000, 2,000, 1,000, and now infrequently, 500, 200 and 100. Coins of 5,000, 2,000, 1,000, 500 and 200 denominations are common in cities but not small towns. Notes from 10,000 to 500,000 are now made of polymer plastic, which ensures a longer life span and makes them difficult to

counterfeit. The dong's value against the dollar has begun to slide in the past few years: at the time of this writing it was about VND12,000 to US$1.

Vietnamese have an obsession with unblemished US dollars and larger dong notes. They will often refuse notes with tears or writing on them, although they can usually be turned in at banks. Counterfeiting of US notes $5 and higher, as well as VND100,000 and higher, is very common.

ATMs

ATM machines are now widely available in most cities. There is a withdrawl limit of VND2,000,000 (just under US$100) per transaction, but the number of transactions is not limited by the ATM. ATM fees are about US$2 per transaction at present.

Travellers' Cheques and Credit Cards

Travellers' cheques in US dollars are accepted in most banks and in major hotels, but not in shops and not in smaller hotels or any restaurants. Major credit cards are accepted at upscale hotels, restaurants, shops and many tour offices.

Tipping and Taxes

Tipping is not expected at restaurants, cafés or hotels run by Vietnamese, if they do not cater mostly to foreign tourists. However, tipping is becoming increasingly common in tourist districts. If service is good, up to 10 percent is recommended. Better hotels may impose a 10 percent tax and 5 percent service charge on receipts, although the tax isn't necessarily forwarded to the government.

P

POLICE

General police are easily identified by their olive-green uniforms with red and yellow highlights and communist emblem on their hats. Traffic police are similarly dressed in tan uniforms. Vietnamese police, in general, are unresponsive and corrupt. 'Tourist Police' in HCMC and Hanoi are generally just for show and do not speak English or have much authority, although they may help you cross busy streets. For any incidents, contact your hotel and go through local police. For serious emergencies you may wish to contact your embassy.

POST

Post offices are generally open every day from 7am to 8pm, and are the telecommunications hub of Vietnam. In the smaller towns, they often don't even identify themselves as post offices *(buu dien)* at all, but rather by the name of the mobile-phone plans (Vinaphone or Mobiphone) they sell. Post offices usually offer computers with internet access

Above from far left: free wifi means fewer internet cafés provide general internet use; Vietnamese banknote.

Maps

Most travel agencies offer free maps of the city in which they are located. Sinh Café Travel has a handy free booklet that includes maps for all the cities they service. Popular bookstores like Fahasa and Phuong Nam sell maps for the cities and provinces in which they are located. Large bookstores in HCMC and Hanoi sell maps and detailed atlases for most parts of the country.

Religion

Vietnam is often called a Buddhist country, but this is a simplistic view. Vietnam is religiously very diverse, and most religious 'Buddhists' practice a mix of Buddhism, Confucianism, Taoism, and a heavy dose of animism and superstition. Foreigners are free to attend government-authorised temples and churches, but their attendance may be noted by authorities, especially at churches. Foreigners who visit unregistered places of worship, or churches in remote areas, may be detained and questioned by local police. Buddhists and Catholics will have no difficulty finding convenient places of worship. Most large towns have at least one Protestant and one Catholic church each. HCMC also has several mosques, Hindu temples, and at least one Chabad Lubavitch (Jewish centre).

(although very slow), fax services, and courier services like FedEx, UPS, DHL and EMS. However, courier services are not as reliable in Vietnam as they might be in other countries. It is common for foreigners to be charged extra for some postal and courier services.

Central Post Offices

Hanoi: 75 Pho Dinh Tien Hoang Street; tel: 04-3825 7036 (domestic), 04-3825 2030 (international).
Ho Chi Minh City: 2 Cong Xa Paris Street; tel: 08-3829 6555.

T

TELEPHONES

When calling a city in Vietnam from overseas, dial the country code 84, followed by the area code but drop the prefix zero. When making a domestic call from one province or city to another in Vietnam, dial the area code first (including the prefix zero). Note: local calls within the same province/city do not require the area code.

Area Codes:

Binh Thuan (Phan Thiet)	062
Lam Dong (Da Lat)	063
Ninh Thuan (Phan Rang)	068
Can Tho	0710
Dak Lak (Buon Ma Thuot)	0500
Danang	0511
HCMC	08
Hanoi	04
Khanh Hoa (Nha Trang)	058
Lao Cai (Sa Pa)	020
Quang Nam (Hoi An)	0510
Quang Ninh	033
Tay Ninh	066
Thua Thien-Hue	054
Vinh Long	070

Country Codes

Australia	0061
Canada	001
Ireland	00353
UK	0044
USA	001

Mobile Phones

Most mobile phone users from overseas who have signed up for roaming facility with their service providers back home will be able to hook up with the GSM 900 or 1800 network that Vietnam uses. The exceptions are users from Japan and North America (unless they have a tri-band phone). Alternatively, cheap phones using prepaid cards can be purchased in Vietnam for a few hundred thousand dong, along with a local number for an additional VND75,000. These prepaid cards are available at Vinaphone and Mobiphone shops, post offices, or any shop that sells mobile phones.

TIME ZONES

Vietnam is seven hours ahead of GMT. It does not observe daylight-saving time.

Above from far left: front-seater cyclos are three-wheeled rickshaws pedalled by drivers; craft workshop.

TRANSPORT

Airports and Arrival

The main international airports are in Ho Chi Minh City (HCMC), Hanoi and Danang. HCMC is the main gateway to the country; fewer international flights go to Hanoi. Danang receives international flights from Singapore, Bangkok and Hong Kong.

Hanoi

Noi Bai International Airport is located about 35km (21 miles) north of downtown Hanoi. It is served by domestic flights as well as international services from Europe, Australia and Asia. There are some 25 airlines serving the airport. For flight information, call Operation Control Centre, tel: 04-3827 1513.

Cover the 35km (21-mile) distance from Noi Bai International Airport to downtown Hanoi in an airport taxi (tel: 04-3873 3333). The trip into town can take anywhere from 40–60 minutes, depending on traffic. The stand is directly outside the Arrivals area; airport taxis charge a fixed rate of US$14 and are exempt from tolls.

Another option is the airport minibus, which costs US$1.80 per person for foreigners and travels directly to Hoan Kiem District. However, the bus only leaves when it is completely full.

Ho Chi Minh City

HCMC's Tan Son Nhat International Airport – just 7km (4 miles) from the city centre – is Vietnam's busiest airport hub, with 32 airlines operating from it and nearly two-thirds of international arrivals and departures into Vietnam using it. For flight information, call the Operation Control Centre, tel: 08-3844 6662/08-3848 5383.

Although Tan Son Nhat International Airport is only 7km (4 miles) northwest of the centre, the ride into town can take up to 30 or 40 minutes. The airport offers few transport options: there are no airport shuttle buses, and it can be overwhelming for visitors with unlicensed taxi 'reps' hassling arrivals for business. The best option is an airport taxi. There are no pre-arranged fixed rates, so be sure to establish the fare before departing (expect to pay around US$10–15 for a ride to downtown HCMC). Note: if you agree to go by meter, some taxi drivers may take long, circuitous routes into town.

Danang

Danang International Airport, the main hub that serves central Vietnam, is located a few kilometres southwest of the city centre. Although designated as an international airport, Danang only receives direct flights from Singapore (Silk Air) and Bangkok (PB Air). Domestic airlines which serve the airport include Vietnam Airlines, Jetstar Pacific Airlines and VASCO. The single-terminal airport is small and with few facilities beyond the basics. For flight information call 0511-382 3377.

Smoking

Smoking is not only common; it is expected of all men beginning their teen years. It is generally considered unfeminine and impolite for women to smoke, though occasionally they do (especially in hill tribes).

Toilets

Most bus trips that cater to foreign tourists include scheduled stops at places that have basic Western-style toilets. Shopping centres, most hotels and the better restaurants and cafés also normally have Western-style toilet facilities. However, go off the beaten tourist track and you're likely to encounter squat toilets. Be sure to carry a pack of tissue paper, as it is unlikely to be available in these situations.

Tourist information
Vietnam's tourism industry lags behind other Asian countries (and for some travellers this may be a good thing). The official representative for Vietnam's tourism – domestically as well as overseas – comes under the purview of the government-operated Vietnam National Administration of Tourism (VNAT; www.vietnamtourism.com). However, it is more involved in the construction of new hotels and infrastructure development than in providing tourist services. State-run 'tourist offices' under the VNAT are merely tour agents out to make money and are not geared towards meeting the requirements of most travellers.

From Danang, places like Hoi An and Hue are easily accessible by road.

By Road

It is possible to enter Vietnam from China at the Lang Son and Lao Cai border crossings in the north. A few travellers travel overland from Laos to Vietnam by bus via the Lao Bao border crossing in central Vietnam. Although definitely not common practice, it is becoming more popular among budget travellers. Travellers also can enter Vietnam by crossing the border with Cambodia at Moc Bai, only a few hours by road from HCMC, or at Vinh Xuong, located about 30km (18 miles) north of Chau Doc in south Vietnam.

Public Transport

Vietnam lacks a well-developed public transport system. The best options are the train system or the private open-tour bus companies.

By Train

Train travel, operated by Vietnam Railways (www.vr.com.vn) in Vietnam, is very slow. Due to the existence of just a single track along the coast, train travel in Vietnam is subject to frequent delays. The fastest express train from Hanoi to HCMC (called the Reunification Express), the SE4 covers 1,730km (1,073 miles) in 29 hours, with the slower ones (like the TBN) taking up to 41 hours because of the numerous stops they make. There are five classes of train travel in Vietnam: hard seat, soft seat, hard sleeper, soft sleeper and soft sleeper with air conditioning – this last option available only on certain trains.

Hanoi's railway station is at 120 Le Duan Street; tel: 04-3942 3697 (located at the far western end of Tran Hung Dao Street). The ticket office is open daily from 7.30–11.30am and 1.30–3.30pm.

Trains leave HCMC for the northern coastal towns from the railway station, which is located at 1 Nguyen Thong Street, District 3 (tel: 08-3843 6528). The ticket office is open daily 7.15am to 11am and 1pm to 3pm.

By Bus

If you are planning to travel long distance by bus, it is best to use one of the comfortable 'Open Tour' air-conditioned bus services. Departing every day, the bus allows you to you to get on or off anywhere along the route from either Hanoi or HCMC (like Hue, Hoi An, Danang, Nha Trang, Da Lat and Mui Ne) with few restrictions. The buses make stops every couple of hours for food and toilet breaks.

Taxis

There are many taxi companies servicing the major cities, and most are renowned for their scams. They can be found waiting on the kerbs of major streets or driving around in circles.

Hanoi: Hanoi Taxi, tel: 04-3853 5353; CP Taxi, tel: 04-3826 2626;

ABC Taxi, tel: 04-3719 1919; Mai Linh Taxi, tel: 04-3822 2555.
Ho Chi Minh City: ML (Mai Linh Taxis/M Taxis), tel: 08-3822 2666; Saigon Tourist, tel: 08-3845 8888; Vina Taxi, tel: 08-3811 1111; Vinasun, tel: 08-3827 2727.

Driving

Despite signing the treaty to participate in the international drivers' permit programme, Vietnam does not honour the agreement. By law, all foreign drivers must possess a Vietnamese driver's licence, which can take more than a month to acquire, thus ruling out driving for most foreign visitors. This said, many tourists do rent motorbikes, though traffic police in the cities have been known to check drivers' licences and confiscate motorbikes.

The best bet for those wishing to take a road trip is to hire a vehicle with driver, easily done at tourist offices or agencies which arrange tours. Check what costs are included and your liability carefully and ensure all involved have signed a contract including your planned itinerary.

V

VISAS AND PASSPORTS

Nationals of 66 countries (at the time of press) are exempt from visas for limited durations when visiting Vietnam. Check the Vietnamese Ministry of Foreign Affairs website at www.mofa.gov.vn for up-to-date information.

For all other nationals, getting a visa is fairly straightforward. Most travellers apply for a one-month, single-entry tourist visa that costs a minimum US$25 (depending upon where you arrange it). Multiple-entry tourist visas have been reduced to three months, starting at $90. However, the Vietnamese Consulate in Sihanoukville, Cambodia, continues regularly to offer visas of longer lengths.

The easy way of getting a visa is to use a travel agent. There will be a commission charge on top of the usual visa processing fee paid to the Vietnamese Embassy or Consulate. In addition to the application form, visitors must submit a valid passport and two passport-size photos. Allow 5–7 working days for approval. Individual travellers may also apply for a visa directly with the Vietnamese Embassy or Consulate in their home country. For a list of Vietnamese foreign missions overseas, check the Ministry of Foreign Affairs website, *right*. Most major tour agents are able to offer pre-arranged visas when you arrive in Hanoi, Danang and HCMC airports, for US$50 or more. The agent will fax applicants an 'invitation letter' to present to immigration on arrival.

The visa period begins on the date specified on the application form – not on the date of entry. Postponing a visit by two weeks means that a month-long visa will only be valid for two weeks.

Above: refuelling. HCMC airport receives more international traffic than Hanoi.

Websites
Vietnam National Administration of Tourism (www.vietnamtourism.com)
Ministry of Foreign Affairs (www.mofa.gov.vn/en)
Local organisation combating the illegal wildlife trade (www.envietnam.org)
Tourism office for Da Lat (www.dalattourist.com.vn)
Tourism site of Halong Bay (www.halong.org.vn)
Government and tourism site for Hanoi (www.hanoi.gov.vn)
HCMC's Department of Tourism (http://tourism.hochiminhcity.gov.vn)
Tourism information in and around Mui Ne Beach (www.muinebeach.net)
Khanh Hoa Province Culture, Sport and Tourism Authority (http://nhatrang-travel.com)

ACCOMMODATION

Hotel development in the country is flourishing and visitors are spoilt for choice. International chains, with service standards and prices to match, can be found in all the major cities. Luxury hotels and resorts with business centres, wifi, and spas and fitness centres, are all par for the course these days, but there is also plenty of choice in the budget lodgings category, where a room can go for about US$10 a night.

When booking your accommodation, always check the hotel website first for comparison. If it's a smaller outfit without a website, call directly to ask for the best rates. The published rates listed here should only be taken as a guide, as actual prices can be quite elastic – depending on seasonal discounts. Higher-end hotels usually charge a 10 percent tax and 5 percent service charge in addition to the listed prices.

During the school holidays (June–August) the beaches get very crowded, and during the annual Tet festival (in late January or early February) buses and trains are packed with domestic travellers. Hotel rates also spike during the Christmas and New Year periods.

Price for a double room for one night without breakfast:

$$$$	Over US$100
$$$	US$50–100
$$	US$20–50
$	Below US$20

If you are making a trip during any of these times, it would be a good idea to book ahead.

Central Highlands

Bao Dai Villa

Lak Lake; tel: 0500-358 6184; www.daklaktourist.com.vn; $

Despite being an old holiday home of the last emperor, all six rooms in the Bao Dai Villa have modern comforts and bathtubs. If available, try for the massive King's Room with his own portraits hung on the walls. The restaurant features black and white photos of the emperor and his elephants.

Damsan Hotel

212–214 Nguyen Cong Tru Street, Buon Ma Thuot; tel: 0500-385 1234; www.damsanhotel.com.vn; $

Damsan is one of the nicest hotels in town, with a pool, tennis court and large restaurant. Service is good, as well as the staff's English, and rooms are comfortable. A lovely coffee shop and bar with balconies sits across the street at Da Quy.

Indochine Dong Duong Hotel

30 Bach Dang Street, Kontum; tel: 060-386 3335; email: indochinevn@kontumtourism.com; $

Indochine is perhaps the best hotel in town. The views of the Dak Bla River and mountains from Indochine are fantastic, the rooms spacious and comfortable. A riverfront pool makes a great

place for evening drinks and watching the sunset. Free breakfast is included.

Da Lat

Da Lat Palace

12 Tran Phu Street, Da Lat; tel: 063-382 5444; www.dalatpalace.vn; $$$$

Da Lat's original luxury hotel (previously managed by Sofitel) is the best choice if you want to be transported back into the time of the French colonials. The hotel originally opened in 1922, and although it was completely renovated in 1995, it still drips with old-world charm and elegance. Rooms are furnished in period French style and have fireplaces.

Evason Ana Mandara Villas Da Lat

Le Loi Street, Da Lat; tel: 063-355 5888; www.anamandara-resort.com; $$$$

This is the most luxurious resort in Da Lat, and is set in an unlikely, secluded neighbourhood on the southwest side of town. The resort's take on rustic elegance is not lost on the 17 beautifully restored French colonial villas dating from the 1920s and 30s. Service and pampering are the focal points, with private butlers assigned to every room.

Da Nang

Furama Resort Da Nang

68 Ho Xuan Huong Street; My An Beach; tel: 0511-384 7888; www.furamavietnam.com; $$$$

Furama is one of Vietnam's premier luxury resorts and located right on China Beach (where American GIs took R&R during the war). The spacious rooms are surrounded by landscaped gardens, and there are two swimming pools and a golf driving range. Furama has a fully equipped fitness centre and several excellent, albeit expensive, restaurants.

Fusion Maia Resort

Son Tra – Dien Ngoc Coastal Street, My Khe Ward; tel: 0511-396 7999; www.fusion-resorts.com; $$$$

The Fusion resorts are a one-of-a-kind luxury experience with unlimited spa treatments included in the price. Each room comes with its own private pool, sunken black granite bathtub, fully loaded iPod and free wifi. The king-sized four-poster beds with swivel widescreen TV (also viewable from the tub) are enough to keep you in the room all day.

Ha Long Bay

Catba Island Resort and Spa

Cat Co 1 Beach, Cat Ba Island; tel: 031-368 8686; www.catbaisland-resort-spa.com; $$$

Set on a hill and surrounded by forest, this plush resort features tastefully outfitted rooms with gorgeous views of the bay and Cat Co Beach. There is also a great free-form pool with waterslides and private beach to lounge away the day. The on-site restaurant serves Asian, Western and seafood dishes.

Above: view over Da Lat.

Point to note
Vietnamese laws insist that all hotel guests be registered with the local police. This generally means leaving your passport with reception the first night.

Hanoi

Church Hotel

9 Nha Tho Street, Hoan Kiem District; tel: 04-3928 8118; www.churchhotel.com.vn; $$

This gem of a boutique hotel, steps away from St Joseph's Cathedral, was built in 2004 and features stylish rooms overlooking trendy Nha Tho Street and the Ba Da Pagoda. Try to get a room facing the back, where it's quieter. All rooms include free wifi and breakfast.

Hanoi Elegance Hotel II

85 Ma May Street, Hoan Kiem District; tel: 04-3926 3451; www.hanoielegancehotel.com; $

Hanoi Elegance is a stylish, modern hotel built in 2006, right in the heart of the Old Quarter. The rooms are large, airy and well furnished; friendly, helpful staff speak good English and are eager to please. The hotel can arrange tours to many of the outlying attractions.

Hilton Hanoi Opera

1 Le Thanh Tong Street, Hoan Kiem District; tel: 04-3933 0500; www.hanoi.hilton.com; $$$$

The Hilton is an architecturally impressive hotel, built to complement the neighbouring Opera House. Rooms are large, airy and modern, and the Vietnamese-style rooms are a particular treat. The wide, spacious lobby features live music and free wifi. The hotel also has a great pool, gym and spa.

Sofitel Legend Metropole Hanoi

15 Ngo Quyen Street, Hoan Kiem District; tel: 04-3826 6919; www.sofitel.com; $$$$

Built in 1901 and renovated by the French Sofitel company in 2005, this grande dame has maintained its colonial-era atmosphere while improving on its comfort levels. Former guests include kings, princes, presidents and an assortment of celebrities. Rooms in both the original Metropole Wing and newer Opera Wing are beautifully appointed, but the latter has larger and more contemporary-style rooms.

Ho Chi Minh City

Caravelle Hotel

19 Lam Son Square, District 1; tel: 08-3823 4999; $$$$

Opened 1959, the 5-star Caravelle is one of the city's most celebrated international hotels, yet it is not part of a generic chain. A glitzy 24-floor edifice, the original low-rise wing was famously home to foreign press corps during the Vietnam War. Past guests have included dignitaries, politicians and celebrities, plus it's a corporate favourite.

Price for a double room for one night without breakfast:

$$$$	Over US$100
$$$	US$50–100
$$	US$20–50
$	Below US$20

Elios

233 Pham Ngu Lao Street, District 1; tel: 08-3838 5585; www.elioshotel.vn; $$

Located in the heart of the backpacker district, this favourite new 3-star hotel has slightly higher standards than others in this price category. The rooms are bright, comfortable and modestly sized; superior rooms are a bit larger. The rooftop restaurant-bar offers good views and is a great place to unwind. Elios also has a gym, meeting rooms and lift.

Lavender Hotel

208–210 Le Thanh Ton Street, District 1; tel: 08-2222 8888; www.lavenderhotel.com.vn; $$$

A much-needed new boutique hotel in this price category, the Lavender Hotel is already a firm favourite for its stylish, intimate ambience and great pricing. Located behind Ben Thanh Market, all rooms are nicely decorated and feature rain showers in the bathrooms and flat-screen TVs (note some rooms don't have windows).

Ordinary Bed and Breakfast

25 Dong Du Street, District 1; tel: 08-3824 8262; email: info@ordinaryvn.com; $

The innovative creation of a Vietnamese-American owner-designer; it's anything but ordinary. This boutique hotel, within a narrow five-storey townhouse, seamlessly blends Indochina furnishings with modern comforts, like a funky coffee bar and contemporary rooms. Thoughtful touches include thick fluffy towels in the rooms.

Hoi An

Life Heritage Resort Hoi An

1 Pham Hong Thai Street; tel: 0510-391 4555; www.life-resorts.com; $$$$

Located on the banks of the Thu Bon River just next to the Old Town, this is one of Hoi An's top resorts. The Senses Restaurant and Vienna Café serve Asian-European fusion cuisine, as well as 'wellness' dishes designed to complement the resort's spa treatments.

Nhat Huy Hoang Hotel

58 Ba Trieu Street; tel: 0510-386 1665; email: nhathuyhoang.coltd@vnn.vn; $

Overall Nhat Huy Hoang is the best value in a city where accommodation is generally overpriced. This small, quiet hotel has friendly, English-speaking staff. The rooms have A/C, satellite TV, hot water, phone and fridge. The hotel is located just a few minutes' walk north of the Old Town.

Hue

Hotel Saigon Morin

30 Le Loi Street; tel: 054-382 3526; www.morinhotel.com.vn; $$$

This historical legend first opened in 1901 and retains much of its old French colonial charm. Conveniently

Above from far left: the Caravelle Hotel; the Catba Resort and Spa has great views over Cat Co Beach *(see p.111)*.

Book ahead
Advanced reservations are highly recommended for upscale hotels in HCMC, Hanoi and Mui Ne, especially during holidays and peak season from mid-December to March. In fact, for Mui Ne, it may be necessary to book a 4–5 star hotel one year in advance for this period.

Something to declare
It's not a good idea to sneak extra people into rooms without presenting their passports. Police do conduct random (and not so random) checks of hotels late at night. Undeclared Vietnamese nationals can be thrown in jail if caught, and foreigners fined significantly.

located across the street from the Perfume River, it's within walking distance of the Dong Ba Market and Royal Citadel. The garden courtyard restaurant serves international cuisine, with a live orchestra playing traditional Vietnamese court music every evening.

La Residence Hotel & Spa

5 Le Loi Street; tel: 054-383 7475; www.la-residence-hue.com; $$$$

This boutique hotel occupies the former home of the French governor. The lovely rooms have three themes: Monuments d'Egypte, Voyage en Chine and Suite d'Ornithologue. Each has Art Deco furnishings, four-poster beds and terraces overlooking the Perfume River and the flagstaff of the Royal Citadel. A spa and fine-dining options are on-site.

Ngoc Binh Hotel

6/34 Nguyen Tri Phuong Street; tel: 054-381 9860; www.ngocbinhhotel.com; $

Conveniently located in the centre of town, the staff is helpful and friendly, and the facilities are disabled-friendly (with a lift system). There is free pick-up from the train and bus stations. Rooms have everything a backpacker could want, including satellite TV, A/C, telephones and hot water.

Price for a double room for one night without breakfast:

$$$$	Over US$100
$$$	US$50–100
$$	US$20–50
$	Below US$20

Mekong Delta

Cuu Long Hotel

1 Road 15, Vinh Long; tel: 070-382 3616; $

There is not a big range of choices for accommodation in Vinh Long, but Cuu Long is the best. It comprises two blocks: A and B. The latter is newer and has more modern facilities. All rooms are spacious and comfortable with en suite bathrooms, and command scenic views over the river.

Victoria Can Tho

Cai Khe Ward, Can Tho; tel: 071-381 0111; www.victoriahotels-asia.com; $$$

This elegant colonial-style resort lies on the banks of the Hau River. Located close to town, but tucked away from the action, all its well-appointed rooms feature furnishings that blend traditional handicrafts with colonial-style design. Balconies look out over the river, pool or gardens.

Nha Trang

Evason Ana Mandara

Tran Phu Street; tel: 058-352 2222; www.sixsenses.com; $$$$

Part of the luxury Six Senses resort chain, the Ana Mandara occupies a slice

of urban beach, albeit a nice one. This elegant property has two swimming pools, two restaurants and two bars, a water sports centre and PADI scuba-diving facility. The villas are beautifully furnished and well appointed.

Sao Mai Hotel

99 Nguyen Thien Thuat Street; tel: 058-352 6412; Saomai2ht@yahoo.com; $

This friendly, family-run hotel is one of the best-value digs in town. The large, tidy rooms have fan or A/C, hot water, fridge and TV. The place is owned by the family of photographer Mai Loc, who leads popular guided tours of central Vietnam.

Panduranga

Ho Phong Hotel

363 Ngo Gia Tu Street, Phan Rang; tel: 068-392 0333; email: hophong@yahoo.com; $

Just off the main drag on the south side of town, Ho Phong is a lovely hotel, with clean and spacious rooms. Rooms have A/C or fans and satellite TV. Complimentary internet access is provided. Minimal English are spoken, but the staff are friendly and do their best to meet your needs.

Mia Resort Mui Ne (Sailing Club)

24 Nguyen Dinh Chieu Street, Mui Ne; tel: 062-384 7440; www.sailingclubvietnam.com; $$$

Mia Resort is part of the renowned Sailing Club chain and a favourite of expats and water sports enthusiasts. Mia offers private bungalows hidden among tropical gardens with a beach-side pool and bar. Xanh Spa, Sandals Restaurant and Storm Kiteboarding are all located on site.

Mui Ne Backpackers (Vietnam-Austria House)

Km 13.5, Mui Ne; tel: 062-384 7047; email: jdajenkins@hotmail.com; $

Previously known as Nha Tro Kim Hong, Vietnam-Austria House and Nhu Huong, Mui Ne Backpackers is one of the oldest local accommodations, and remains a backpacker favourite to this day. Dorms, private rooms and beachside bungalows are all on offer, with a swimming pool out front.

Sa Pa

Victoria Sapa Resort

Sa Pa Town; tel: 020-387 1522; www.victoriahotels-asia.com; $$$$

This charming chalet-style resort is located just above the town, and offers stunning views of the valley and Mount Fansipan. Rooms are warm and luxurious with unique Vietnamese accents. The property features a beautiful pool, garden and spa. The resort can arrange its own train transfers on board the exclusive Victoria Express from Hanoi.

Above from far left: enjoy the view at Evason Ana Mandara; the Victoria Can Tho.

RESTAURANTS

Vietnam has seen an explosion of new restaurants oriented towards foreign visitors and affluent locals in the last few years. Most of the action in this new food scene is in Hanoi and HCMC (watch for a new Bobby Chinn Restaurant in District 1, HCMC sometime in 2011–12), with significant development also in Mui Ne and Nha Trang. That being said, the traditional cuisine in the north and south, as well as Hue and Hoi An, should certainly not be ignored. Don't be afraid to try street vendors and market stalls. Street food is delicious, inexpensive and generally quite safe, though you may wish to avoid ice in your drinks and wipe your chopsticks and silverware before use.

The restaurants listed in this guide generally cluster together within a single area in each city (the area of most interest to tourists). The exceptions are HCMC, where restaurants are located around both Pham Ngu Lao and Dong Khoi streets, and in Hanoi, where good dining options are available in the Old Quarter, French Quarter and West Lake (Tay Ho).

Da Lat

Café Nam Huy

26 Phan Dinh Phung Street; tel: 063-352 0205; B, L, D; $

Located in walking distance from the backpacker district but frequented by locals, this cosy café has lots of sitting nooks surrounded by aquariums. Nam Huy serves great street dishes like *pho* and beef curry, all for under US$1. Outdoor seating is also available.

Phu Dong

1A/1B Quang Trung Street; tel: 063-354 2222; B, L, D; $$$

Ambience is the draw here in this French-style castle. The beautiful stonework, mosaic floors and fountains offer a romantic departure from typical Vietnamese restaurants. Classical music serenades you as you are treated to traditional Vietnamese cuisine and local specialities. Indoor and outdoor seating is available.

Whynot Café

24 Nguyen Chi Thanh Street; tel: 063-383 2540; B, L, D; $$

The classiest of the Vietnamese cafés in town, Whynot sits above the Central Market and has a menu that includes Western favourites like burgers, pasta and pizza. The selection of drinks is vast. A flat-screen TV on each floor shows American films and cable television. There's also free wifi.

Da Nang

Apsara Restaurant

222 Tran Phu Street; tel: 0511-356 1409; L, D; $$$

This upscale restaurant near the Cham museum serves fresh seafood and local delicacies with a Cham theme. You'll pass a recreated Cham tower in miniature (although it still looms high above) as you enter. Nightly tra-

ditional Cham music and dance shows are scheduled from 6.30–8pm.

Garden View Café

37 Le Dinh Duong Street; tel: 0511-358 2482; www.truclamvien.com.vn; B, L, D; $

The owners of the popular Pho 24 and Com Nieu chains throughout Vietnam own this truly unique café, set in four ancient wooden houses. There is a central garden with waterfalls and goldfish ponds. Prices are higher than a typical Da Nang café, but the food is exceptional. Breakfast is the main draw.

Hanoi

Alfresco's

23L Hai Ba Trung Street; tel: 04-3826 7782; 98 Xuan Dieu Street; tel: 043-719 5322; B, L, D; $$$

This is the place if you crave quality, upmarket fast food. This family-oriented restaurant is popular for its jumbo ribs, imported Australian steaks and burgers, fish and chips, plus decent Mexican dishes, all with generous portions. This expat favourite has two locations.

Cost of a meal for one including up to three dishes and a drink:

$$$$	Over US$10
$$$	US$6–10
$$	US$2.50–5
$	Under US$2.50

Green Tangerine

48 Hang Be Street; tel: 04-3825 1286; L, D; $$$$

The Green Tangerine is set in a gorgeous restored French villa in the heart of the Old Quarter. Lounge in the atmospheric interior, or dine in the garden courtyard. The French chef creates mouth-watering international fusion as well as traditional French with innovative twists.

Highway 4 Bar & Restaurant

5 Hang Tre Street; tel: 04-3926 0639; 54 Mai Hac De Street; tel: 04-3976 2647; L, D; $$$

Highway 4 specialises in exotic rice wine liquors and North Vietnamese cuisine, especially hotpot, fish, spring rolls (try the catfish spring rolls with wasabi-based dip) and carmelised clay pot dishes. Amid traditional northern decor, sit cross-legged at low split-bamboo tables. The roof terrace is recommended. Two Hanoi locations.

Le Tonkin

14 Ngo Van So Street; tel: 04-3943 3457; B, L, D; $$

Set in a century-old restored French villa, filled with regional antiquities and ambience. Dine inside or in the courtyard. The beautifully presented Vietnamese cuisine is modified to suit Westerners. Evening traditional music performances on Mondays and Fridays are a bonus. Le Tonkin is great value for money.

Above from far left: Hanoi's dining scene extends from smart restaurants to casual backpacker haunts.

Vegetarianism
Vietnamese do not have the same definition of vegetarian that is understood in the West. 'Vegetarian' dishes may still contain pork fat or fish sauce. The best places to find vegetarian food are in stalls outside active pagodas.

Nut allergies
Peanuts are a common ingredient in Vietnamese cuisine, particularly in dipping sauces. If you do not want peanuts in your food (for example, if you have a peanut allergy), you may request 'Lam on khong cho toi dau phong' (Please don't give me peanuts).

Quan An Ngon

18 Phan Boi Chau Street; tel: 04-3942 8162; B, L, D; $$$

This successful HCMC venture has found equal success in Hanoi. Sit at simple tables set in a pretty alfresco villa courtyard and enjoy traditional Vietnamese dishes served from the surrounding mock street food stalls. The restaurant can get very busy, but is open all day.

Wild Rice

6 Ngo Thi Nham Street; tel: 04-3943 8896; L, D; $$$$

This stunning restaurant incorporates both Japanese and minimalist design influences. The contemporary Vietnamese dishes – reinvented for Western tastes – is flavoursome and great value. Wild Rice is a favourite of expats, and the sort of place they tend to take visiting friends and relatives to show off a bit.

Ho Chi Minh City

Barbecue Garden

135A Nam Ky Khoi Nghia Street, District 1; tel: 08-3823 3340; www.barbecuegarden.com; D only; $$$

This party favouite is situated in a large garden setting, underneath trees swathed in fairy lights. Clay pots with coals are set on each table so that you can barbecue your own skewered meats (pork, beef, chicken and seafood) and vegetables, best eaten wrapped in rice paper with fresh herbs.

Ben Thanh Night Market

Phan Boi Chau and Phan Chu Trinh streets, District 1; D only; $–$$$

Post-dusk, open-air, makeshift eateries assembled outside Ben Thanh Market which serve a huge selection of good-value Vietnamese fare. The streets are packed nightly with locals and tourists in an ideal spot to sample local street food. Dishes include noodle soups, seafood crêpes, fruit salads and shakes and plenty of seafood.

Com Nieu Saigon

6C Tu Xuong Street, District 1; tel: 08-3932 6388; L, D; $$$

Com Nieu is popular for its flavoursome southern cuisine and entertaining spectacle of waiters smashing clay pots of charcoal-grilled rice *(com dap)* and throwing the extracted contents across the room. This otherwise traditional restaurant was a favourite of Anthony Bourdain.

The Refinery

74 Hai Ba Trung Street, District 1; tel: 08-3823 0509; D; $$$$

This period French-style bistro is housed in a restored opium refinery, set off the street, behind the Opera House. The menu features a selection of contemporary European dishes and includes home-made ice creams, as well as excellent weekend brunches. Unsurprisingly, the Refinery is a favourite evening hideaway for expats.

Square One

Mezzanine, Park Hyatt Saigon, 2 Lam Son Square, District 1; tel: 08-3520 2357; www.saigon.park.hyatt.com; B, L, D; $$$$

Hyatt's signature restaurant features five show kitchen stations. The menu includes simple yet top-notch Western and Vietnamese dishes, a variety of grilled, steamed and wok-fried food. Steaks and seafood are among the house specialities. After dinner, head to the Hyatt's 2 Lam Son Bar, the most cosmopolitan bar in town.

Temple Club

29–31 Ton That Thiep Street, District 1; tel: 08-3829 9244; L, D; $$$$

Housed within a former Hindu pilgrim guesthouse, the refined interiors evoke Saigon's old Indochina and almost, but not entirely, overshadow the traditional Vietnamese cuisine. This is a good restaurant to head for a special occasion requiring a romantic atmosphere.

Hoi An

Good Morning Vietnam

34 Le Loi Street; tel: 0510-391 0227; www.goodmorningviet.com; L, D; $$$

Despite no serious Italian competition in Hoi An, Good Morning Vietnam offers consistently good service and quality pastas, pizza and traditional cuisine from imported Italian chefs, making this restaurant chain a favourite in every city it colonises throughout Vietnam.

Cost of a meal for one including up to three dishes and a drink:

$$$$	Over US$10
$$$	US$6–10
$$	US$2.50–5
$	Under US$2.50

Omar Khayyam's

24 Tran Hung Dao Street; tel: 0510-386 4538; B, L D; $$$

This popular chain of Indian restaurants in Vietnam has brought spice and much needed variety to the Hoi An food scene. Omar is located just outside the Old Town, so you can walk or drive there. The menu features lots of curry, tandoori and vegetarian options.

Hue

JASS Japanese Restaurant

12 Chu Van An Street; tel: 054-382 8177; D only; $$$

The menu is small but the dishes are developed to perfection with flavours that are clean and delicate. The Japanese Association of Supporting Street Children, founded by Michio Koyama, runs an excellent programme with the stated aim of housing, educating and training disadvantaged youth. This restaurant is one of the newest extensions of the programme which

Above from far left: opulent decor at a café in HCMC; a typical Hoi An dish.

has changed the lives of hundreds of young people.

Omar Khayyam's

10 Nguyen Tri Phuong Street; tel: 054-382 1616; 22 Pham Ngu Lao Street; tel: 054-381 0310; L, D; $$$

Omar's is so successful – and deservedly so – that it has two locations in Hue, one in each of the tourist spots. Pham Ngu Lao is a livelier location with flashier decor (and overall better food). The tandoori and curry is consistently excellent. Their pot of chai is a great bargain too.

Phuong Nam Café

38 Tran Cao Van Street; tel: 054-384 9317; B, L, D; $

Despite lots of foreign customers, prices have remained normal (cheap) and the menu entirely Vietnamese, except for the many pancakes. Service is slow but friendly. Try the *bun thit nuong* (grilled meat and noodles) or the many Hue specialities.

Nha Trang

Da Fernando

96 Nguyen Thien Thuat Street; tel: 058-322 9102; L, D; $$$

Fernando formerly helmed Good Morning Vietnam in Mui Ne, but has come into his own in Nha Trang. The menu includes popular favourites – pizza, pasta, gnocchi and risotto – but moves beyond the basics for delightful surprises. Anchovies, sun-dried tomatoes and highly refined olive oil are signature speciality ingredients.

La Mancha

78 Nguyen Thien Thuat Street; tel: 091-456 9782; B, L, D; $$$

La Mancha has the most attentive and cheerful service of any restaurant in the tourist district. This excellent tapas restaurant has a great atmosphere, lively Spanish music and a fountain at the centre. Free fresh bread keeps coming throughout the meal. Try the stewed Spanish sausages.

Omar's

98A/8 Tran Phu Street; tel: 058-352 2459; 98B Nguyen Thien Thuat Street; tel: 058-322 1615; B, L, D; $$$

With two locations in Nha Trang, you know it's got to be good. Master chef Omar from New Delhi serves a superb mix of meat and vegetarian curries, tandoori barbecues, Indian breads and rice. Omar's is a polished restaurant with the friendliest service of any of the franchises.

La Taverna

115 Nguyen Thien Thuat Street; tel: 058-352 2259; L, D; $$$

Swiss-Italian owner Athos was the original manager of Good Morning Vietnam Nha Trang and has graduated to a fine restaurant serving all the popular Italian basics (pizzas, pastas,

lasagne, gnocchi, ravioli and tagliatelle) as well as select dishes from Switzerland like polenta and spezzatini.

Panduranga

Champa Restaurant

Coco Beach Resort, 58 Nguyen Dinh Chieu Street, Mui Ne; tel: 062-384 7111/2/3; D only; $$$$

Offering French *cuisine bourgeoise*, Champa offers some of the finest food in the area. The restaurant is decorated with crafts from the local Cham minority, and the large terrace overlooks the pool and gardens. The bar serves great cocktails, Cuban cigars and French tunes.

Good Morning Vietnam

57 Nguyen Dinh Chieu, Mui Ne; tel: 062-384 7585; www.goodmorningviet.com; B, L, D; $$$

Italian-owned and managed, this Vietnam restaurant chain is a favourite of expats and travellers alike. Pizzas are their claim to fame, but their breads (free with every meal), pastas and meat dishes are exceptional. Free transport to and from your hotel is available.

Cost of a meal for one including up to three dishes and a drink

$$$$	Over US$10
$$$	US$6–10
$$	US$2.50–5
$	Under US$2.50

Shree Ganesh

57 Nguyen Dinh Chieu Street, Mui Ne; tel: 062-374 1330; B, L, D; $$$

Part of a chain in Vietnam, this popular venue serves North Indian and tandoori cuisine to the sounds of lively Indian music. Curry is understandably king here, and the author hasn't found a dish yet on the menu that he doesn't like.

Snow

109 Nguyen Dinh Chieu Street, Mui Ne; tel: 062-743 123; B, L, D; $$

This Russian-owned restaurant, club and sushi bar, set in the centre of the beach, is one of the trendiest spots in town. The all-white decor offset by a deep-blue ceiling is particularly striking. Snow is a great evening hangout for gourmet seafood and cocktails. Free pick-up from your hotel is available.

Sa Pa

Ta Van Restaurant

Victoria Sapa Resort, Sa Pa Town; tel: 020-387 1522; www.victoriahotels-asia.com; $$$$

Dine inside the lodge by the fireplace or outside on the terrace with views of Mount Fansipan. The menus include European and Asian favourites, with emphasis on Vietnamese and Cambodian cuisine (the latter is strangely uncommon in Vietnam). Live ethnic music and dance is performed in the evenings.

Above: Hue cuisine.

Extra charges

Anything that is placed on the table but not ordered will usually appear on the bill as an additional charge. The only exceptions are usually ice tea (but not always), and bread at Italian or upscale restaurants. Hotels and better restaurants may charge an additional 10 percent tax and 5 percent service charge to the bill as well.

NIGHTLIFE

Vietnam's nightlife scene has vastly improved over the last few years, though recent visitors to neighbouring Bangkok or Singapore may find themselves underwhelmed. The most activity is located in HCMC and Hanoi, with a burgeoning scene in Nha Trang and Mui Ne. Vietnam's 'culture police' (no joke, they do exist) have laid off lately, allowing venues to stay open later (larger clubs tend to close at midnight, but smaller venues are open later, and a rare few stay open all night). New noise level laws in 2011, specifically aimed at entertainment venues located near hotels, may make the situation complicated. Dance clubs and bars tend to cluster around the hotels and restaurants that serve tourists and affluent locals, but cultural venues are more spread around the cities. The selections below represent some of the highlights.

Hanoi

Cheo Hanoi Theatre

15 Nguyen Dinh Chieu Street, Hai Ba Trung District; tel: 04-3943 7361

Cheo theatre is a uniquely northern Vietnamese folk art that originated in the Red River Delta. The shows – which incorporate dance, music and drama – depict the ordinary struggles and successes of rural Vietnamese, and often without English translation.

Dragonfly

15 Hang Buom Street, Hoan Kiem District; tel: 04-3926 2177; www.dragonfly.vn

A lively Hanoi favourite with a long history, Dragonfly features good drinks, a dance floor and an upstairs shisha lounge. Dragonfly welcomes a wide mix of patrons, with nightly drinks specials.

Opera House

1 Trang Tien Street; Hoan Kiem District; tel: 04-3993 0113; www.ticketvn.com

Built in the early 1900s by the French, Hanoi's Opera House holds regular performances of classical and traditional music, as well as dance, by local and foreign artists of note. The performance space is quite small, making for an intimate evening.

Le Pub

25 Hang Be Street, Hoan Kiem District; tel: 04-3926 2104; www.lepub.org

This is one of those places where travellers, expats and locals mix easily. The location in the Old Quarter is excellent, the music is up to date, there are nightly drinks specials, the food is diverse and good, and the staff are very friendly.

R&R Tavern

47 Lo Su Street, Hoan Kiem District; tel: 04-3934 4109; www.rockandroll tavern-hanoi.com

Probably the first American-run joint

in Hanoi, R&R Tavern opened in 1995 and has established itself as the classic American bar in the capital. Spacious and airy, the downstairs bar area features live bands, while upstairs has more of a lounge feel. R&R serves some of the city's best Mexican food.

Ho Chi Minh City

Apocalypse Now

2B Thi Sach Street, District 1; tel: 08-3825 6124

Saigon just has to have a club by this name. This long-running institution is by turns adored, despised and occasionally shut down. The name says it all and, like the movie, you may just lose your mind here. Apocalypse plays hip dance music and features occasional live bands.

Ho Chi Minh City Conservatory of Music

112 Nguyen Du Street, District 1; tel: 08-3824 3774; www.hbso.org.vn

Founded in 1956, the conservatory is southern Vietnam's centre for classical (Western) music training, closely affiliated with the Ho Chi Minh City Ballet, Symphony, Orchestra and Opera (HBSO). Occasional classical music performances hosted here.

Lush

2 Ly Trong Street, District 1; tel: 08-824 2496

Established by a San Francisco native, this is one of HCMC's hippest, hottest nightclubs, heaving most nights with a diverse and party-ready crowd comprised of both locals and foreigners. Decorated in lounge style with an intimate feel, Lush offers an infectious party atmosphere and cool sounds from cutting-edge DJs. The upstairs balcony is a poser's paradise.

Municipal Theatre

7 Lam Son Square, District 1; tel: 08-3829 9976; www.hbso.org.vn; box office: 8am–8pm performance day, otherwise Mon–Sat 8am–5.30pm; tickets: tel: 08-3925 2265

The grand Municipal Theatre (Opera House), opened in 1899 and renovated a century later, is mainly used by the Ho Chi Minh City Ballet, Symphony, Orchestra and Opera (HBSO) and visiting artists. Classical dance and music performances, including concerts, are held every month on the 9th and 19th.

Sax n' art

28 Le Loi Street, District 1; tel: 08-3822 8472; www.saxnart.com

HCMC's premier jazz and blues club is a suave, intimate venue, with black-and-white photos and vintage saxophones displayed on the walls. Live performances nightly (after 9pm), featuring well-known saxophonist-owner Tran Manh Tuan with his house band, plus occasional international guest musicians.

Above: visit Lush in HCMC for DJs playing pop and hip hop to a mixed crowd of locals and tourists.

Stay safe

Nightlife in Vietnam is generally a very safe experience but precautions necessary in other countries should also be observed here. Don't accept opened drinks from strangers. Women should be careful leaving bars late at night with male moto taxi drivers, especially if they have consumed alcohol. Be careful of valuables. Snatch-and-drive thieves often wait for patrons exiting bars.

CREDITS

Insight Step by Step Vietnam
Written by: Adam Bray
Series Editor: Sarah Sweeney
Map Production: original cartography by Lovell Johns, updated by Stephen Ramsay and APA Cartography department
Production: Tynan Dean and Linton Donaldson
Picture Manager: Steven Lawrence
Art Editor: Ian Spick

Photography: All pictures copyright APA/Peter Stuckings, except: APA/Julian Abram Wainwright 23B; Six Senses Resorts and Spas 114; Victoria Hotels & Resorts 115
Front cover: main image: Corbis; bottom left: iStockphoto; bottom right: iStockphoto
Back cover: (both) APA/Peter Stuckings

Printed by: CTPS – China

First Edition 2011

CONTACTING THE EDITORS

We would appreciate it if readers would alert us to errors or outdated information by writing to us at insight@apaguide.co.uk or APA Publications, PO Box 7910, London SE1 1WE, UK.

www.insightguides.com

DISTRIBUTION

Worldwide
APA Publications GmbH & Co. Verlag KG (Singapore branch)
7030 Ang Mo Kio Ave 5
08-65 Northstar @ AMK, Singapore 569880
Email: apasin@singnet.com.sg

UK and Ireland
GeoCenter International Ltd
Meridian House, Churchill Way West
Basingstoke, Hampshire RG21 6YR
Email: sales@geocenter.co.uk

United States
Ingram Publisher Services
One Ingram Blvd, PO Box 3006
La Vergne, TN 37086-1986
Email: customer.service@ingrampublisher services.com

Australia
Universal Publishers
PO Box 307
St. Leonards NSW 1590
Email: sales@universalpublishers.com.au

INDEX

I

K

L

M

Hanoi
0
500 m
0
500 yds
N
Au Co
TAY HO
Chua Phu Tay Ho (West Lake Pagoda)
Ngo 31
Xuan Dieu
Au Co
Chua Kim Lien (Golden Lotus Pagoda)
Sheraton Hotel
Intercontinental Westlake Hotel
Yen Phu
Nghi Tam
An Duong
An Duong
Ho Tay
(West Lake)
Chua Tran Quoc (Pagoda)
Pho Duc Chinh
Truc Bach
Chua Ngu Xa (Pagoda)
Ngu Xa
Ho Truc Bach (White Silk Lake)
Thanh Nien
Nghia Dung
Co Xa
Phuc Xa
Tan Ap
Yen Phu
Nguyen Khac Nhu
Pham Hong Thai
Nguyen Truong To
Dang Dung
Chau Long
Cua Bac
Den Quan Thanh (Temple)
Tran Vu
Quan Thanh
Ng. Bieu
Thuy Khue
Hoang Hoa Tham
Cua Bac (Catholic Church)
Chua Noe Nhai
Hoe Nhai
Phuc Xa
Phan Dinh Phung
Ga Long Bien (Station)
Cau Long Bien
Hang Dau
Gam Cau
Tran
CONG VIEN BACH THAO (BOTANICAL GARDEN)
Nha San Bac Ho (Ho Chi Minh's House)
Ng. Canh Chan
Hoang Van Thu
Ba Dinh Square
OLD CITY
CITADEL
36 PHO PHUONG
Cho Dong Xuan (Market)
BA DINH
Phu Chu Tich (Presidential Palace)
Lang Chu Tich Ho Chi Minh (Ho Chi Minh Mausoleum)
Ho Huu Tiep (B-52 Lake)
Chua Mot Cot (One Pillar Pagoda)
Bao Tang Chien Thang B-52 (B-52 Museum)
Vuong
Hung
13
Bac Son
Hoang Dieu
Nguyen Tri Phuong
Military Area (Restricted Access)
Cua Dong
Ly Nam De
H. Cot
H. Luoc
D. Xuan
H. Chieu
Den Bach Ma
H. Buom
Nhat Duat
Phuc Tan
(OLD QUARTER)
Hang Ga
Thuoc Bac
Hang Bo
Hang Bac
Nha Hat Chuong
Nha Hat Mu (Water Puppe
Doi Can
Bao Tang Ho Chi Minh (Ho Chi Minh Museum)
Chua Mot Cot
Bao Tang Lich Su Quan Su Viet Nam (Military History Museum)
Le Hong Phong
Ong Ich Khiem
Son Tay
Kim Ma
Tran Phu
Chu Van An
Khuc Hao
Lenin
Dien Bien Phu
Phung Hung
Bat Dan
H. Quat
H. Gai
Cau Go
12
Den Ngoc Son
Ho Hoan Kiem
Thap Rua
Le Thai To
Dinh Tien Hoang
Tran Ng
Nguyen Thai Hoc
Bao Tang My Thuat (Fine Arts Museum)
Giang Vo
Trinh Hoai Duc
Bao Tang Dan Toc Hoc Viet Nam (Vietnam Museum of Ethnology)
Ciputra International City
Cat Linh
Van Mieu (Temple of Literature)
P. Van Mieu
P. Nguyen Khuyen
Hang Bong
Ly Quoc Su
H. Da
Nha Tho Lon (St Joseph's Cathedral)
Nha Chung
Trang Thi
12
Ngo Bai
Quoc Tu Giam
D. Thi Diem
Ngo Si Lien
Tran Quy Cap
Phan Boi Chau
Tho Nhuom
Ba Tang Nha Bao Hoa Lo (Prison Museum "Hanoi Hilton")
H. Khay
Trang Tien
Hang Bot
N. Thong Phong
Ga Ha Noi (Station)
Chua Quan Su (Ambassadors' Pagoda)
Ly Thuong Kiet
Hai Ba Trung
Ngo Hao Nam
Ngo Thinh Hao 1
N. Van Huong
Ton Duc Thang
Ngo Luong
Ba Trieu
Quyen
Le Duan
Cung Van Hoa Huu Nghi (Cultural Palace)
Ngo Van Chuong
Ngo Quan Tho 1
Yet Kieu
Tran Binh Trong
Tran Quoc Toan
Tran Hung Dao
Ngo
La Thanh
Thien Hung
Nguyen Du
Quang Trung
Nguyen Du
Ham Long
Hue
Ngo Thi Nham
Nha Hat Tuoi Tre
Kham Thien
Ng. Thuong Hien
Ho Thien Quang
DONG DA
Ngo Chu Kham Thien
Tran Nhan Tong
Ng. Binh Khiem
Tran Xuan Soan
Ngo Xa Dan
Nguyen Luong Bang
De La Thanh
Nha Hat Rap Xiec (Circus Theatre)
Nha Hat Cheo (Cheo Theatre)
Nha Hat Dai Nam
Tue Tinh
Hoa Ma
CONG VIEN THONG NHAT (REUNIFICATION PARK)
Ng. D. Chieu
Ba Trieu
Nguyen Cong Tru
Go Dong Da
Den Hai Ba Trung
Thu Dau Mot
Bien Hoa
Huynh M Dat
Xo Viet
Rach Thi Nghe
Chua Ngoc Hoang (Jade Emperor Pagoda)
Tran Quang Khai
Nguyen Phi Khanh
Tran Khanh Du
Tran Qui Khoach
Dang Dung
Nguyen Huu Canh
Dinh Phung
Song (Red R